全国教育学系列规划教材

教育英语阅读教程
Selected English Readings for Education

主 编 杨洪艳 祝 平

苏州大学出版社

图书在版编目(CIP)数据

教育英语阅读教程 = Selected English Readings for Education / 杨洪艳,祝平主编. —苏州:苏州大学出版社,2022.5
全国教育学系列规划教材
ISBN 978-7-5672-3936-4

Ⅰ.①教… Ⅱ.①杨…②祝… Ⅲ.①英语-阅读教学-高等学校-教材 Ⅳ.①H319.37

中国版本图书馆 CIP 数据核字(2022)第 067441 号

书　　名：	教育英语阅读教程
	Selected English Readings for Education
主　　编：	杨洪艳　祝　平
责任编辑：	汤定军
策划编辑：	汤定军
封面设计：	刘　俊
出版发行：	苏州大学出版社(Soochow University Press)
社　　址：	苏州市十梓街1号　邮编:215006
印　　装：	广东虎彩云印刷有限公司
网　　址：	www.sudapress.com
邮　　箱：	sdcbs@suda.edu.cn
邮购热线：	0512-67480030
销售热线：	0512-67481020
开　　本：	787 mm×1 092 mm　1/16　印张:12　字数:278千
版　　次：	2022年5月第1版
印　　次：	2022年5月第1次印刷
书　　号：	ISBN 978-7-5672-3936-4
定　　价：	48.00元

凡购本社图书发现印装错误,请与本社联系调换。服务热线:0512-67481020

编者的话

苏州科技大学(原铁道部直属苏州铁道师范学院与原建设部直属苏州城建环保学院2001年合并而成)英语师范(英语教育)本科专业1985年开始招生,是当时江苏省实施英语师范本科教育的五所院校之一,至今已连续招生近40届。该专业40年弦歌不断,砥砺奋进,积淀深厚,成就斐然,曾于2012年入选"十二五"江苏省高等学校本科重点专业,并于2019年被遴选为江苏省一流本科专业及江苏省特色专业建设点。

近年来,我们以江苏省重点专业建设、江苏省一流专业(特色专业)建设为依托,以江苏省教改课题和江苏省社科应用研究精品工程课题研究为抓手,积极探索新时代卓越中小学英语教师培养的有效路径。课程设置必然是人才培养过程中考量的重要维度。因此,在制定英语师范专业人才培养方案时,我们重构了课程体系,加大了师范职业养成类课程的比例,并以"基于内容的教学"(Content-Based Instruction, CBI)理念为指导,用英语讲授教师教育教学类课程,既注重打好英语师范生的英语语言基本功,也传输英语教育教学知识和培养其教育教学能力。

"教育经典阅读"就是这样一门课程,它替代了传统的"英语阅读"课程。我们希望这门课程除了完成传统的英语阅读课教学任务之外,还能让英语师范生对教育学理论有一个初步的了解,以便为未来的英语教学理论课程学习乃至未来的教育教学打下一定的理论基础,使学生知道英语教学相关理论的最初出处,知晓流行的教育思想的起源,让学生在学习教育教学理论的时候既不会觉得理论与教学相去甚远,又不会当看到一个新的理论出现的时候就奉若神明,而是能够追溯到理论原点,并批判性地学习和运用。

这本《教育英语阅读教程》以CBI理念为支撑来选择和设计课文及练习。本教程共10个单元,每个单元由两篇主题相关的课文及相关练习构成。前两个单元内容分别是4位美国学者对美国中小学和大学教育中倡导的"批判性思维"的反思。通过这两个单元的学习,学生可以客观、理性地看待西方国家教育优缺点,理解中国教育问题产生的原因以及中国教育的优势,最终做到当面对国外纷繁复杂的教育理论时能够审慎思考,"取其精华,去其糟粕",使这些理论扎根于中国的教育现实,真正做到把这些教育理论本土化。

第3单元至第10单元分别是柏拉图、夸美纽斯、赫尔巴特、洛克、卢梭、斯宾塞、杜威、布鲁纳等教育名著的节选。其中,第3单元和第8单元的第2篇课文则分别是《论语》和陶行知论著的节选。这几个单元旨在帮助师范生了解重要的中外教育家教育哲学思想的

I

最核心内容,增强学生对教育思想的理解,提高学生对教学理论学习的兴趣。当然,这些教育名家的教育思想和教育主张也是教师资格考试的重点内容。

每单元设计了以下练习:课文学习前的提问、对课文内容的提问、针对课文重要词汇的填空练习、对课文难句的翻译、对课文内容的正误判断、用课文中词汇和语句进行的翻译练习、对课文句子的英文解释练习、对学习策略的介绍及相关练习等。此外,每个单元还设计了与两篇课文内容相关以及以提高学生语言运用能力、教育思想运用能力和合作学习能力的综合项目训练。练习设计层层递进,兼顾教育思想理解和语言能力的提高。课前提问可以引发学生推测课文内容,提高学生学习课文的兴趣;课后语言练习可以提升学生与教育哲学话题相关的英语语言能力;学习策略练习可以提升学生策略意识,让学生在英语学习中自觉使用各种适合自己的学习策略,提高学习效率。项目练习则通过调查、讨论、写小报告等形式在加强学生语言运用能力的同时,提高学生逻辑思辨能力,加深学生对教育思想的理解。

本教程可以用作英语师范专业本科生阅读教材,也可以作为其他师范专业的专业英语教材,或教育学和学科教学硕士的研究生英语教材。学习本教程的学生可以增加教育类词汇的积累,提升阅读教育经典原著的能力,养成通过阅读教育经典来了解教育家教育思想的良好习惯,为未来的教育教学工作打下良好的基础。

本教程由杨洪艳和祝平合作编写。杨洪艳负责课文选材和练习编写工作,祝平负责全书结构及单元结构设计和统稿工作。

本教程为"十二五"江苏省重点本科专业(苏教高函〔2012〕23号)建设、江苏省一流本科专业/特色专业(苏教高函〔2020〕9号)建设、江苏省社科应用研究精品工程外语类重点课题"新文科背景下卓越英语教师职前培养体系研究"(19SWA-002)成果,得到这些项目经费资助。

苏州大学出版社汤定军老师为本书出版付出了艰辛的劳动,在此谨致谢忱!

编者

2022年1月31日辛丑年除夕

Contents

Unit 1　**Critical Thinking**
- Text 1　Critical Thinking: Not All That Critical　/ 2
- Text 2　On Critical Thinking　/ 13
- Learning Strategies　/ 19
- Unit Project　/ 20

Unit 2　**Liberal Arts**
- Text 1　Who Killed the Liberal Arts?　/ 22
- Text 2　The Danger of Liberal Arts Education?　/ 31
- Learning Strategies　/ 38
- Unit Project　/ 39

Unit 3　**Ancient Educational Wisdom**
- Text 1　Republic　/ 41
- Text 2　The Analects　/ 52
- Learning Strategies　/ 58
- Unit Project　/ 59

Unit 4　**Teaching and Learning Principles**
- Text 1　The Principles of Facility and Thoroughness in Teaching and Learning　/ 61
- Text 2　The Principles of Conciseness and Rapidity in Teaching　/ 70
- Learning Strategies　/ 77
- Unit Project　/ 77

Unit 5　**Respecting Children**
- Text 1　Some Thoughts Concerning Education　/ 79
- Text 2　Emile, or on Education　/ 88
- Learning Strategies　/ 95
- Unit Project　/ 95

Unit 6　**Steps in Instruction or Thinking**
- Text 1　Steps in Instruction　/ 97
- Text 2　The Five Logical Steps　/ 107
- Learning Strategies　/ 115
- Unit Project　/ 116

Unit 7　**Why Should Science Be Taught in Schools?**
- Text 1　What Knowledge Is of Most Worth?　/ 118

I

- Text 2　Science and Education　/ 125
- Learning Strategies　/ 133
- Unit Project　/ 133

Unit 8　Life as Education
- Text 1　The Conception of Educational Development　/ 135
- Text 2　Creative Education　/ 144
- Learning Strategies　/ 150
- Unit Project　/ 150

Unit 9　Punishments and Rewards
- Text 1　The Way to Discipline Kids　/ 152
- Text 2　Corporal Punishments and Rewards　/ 162
- Learning Strategies　/ 169
- Unit Project　/ 169

Unit 10　The Way to Promote Retention
- Text 1　Meaningful Learning　/ 171
- Text 2　The Process of Education　/ 180
- Learning Strategies　/ 185
- Unit Project　/ 186

Unit 1

Critical Thinking

Pre-reading questions:

1. What is critical thinking?
2. How do we cultivate critical thinking ability?

Text 1

Critical Thinking: Not All That Critical

Bruce Dietrick Price

1. Critical Thinking, unless you are a **snarling**[1] pit bull of irrationality, is an infinitely glorious thing. Well, that's what our public schools are telling kids and parents. Critical Thinking is said to be **synonymous**[2] with fairness, **impartiality**[3], science, logic, maturity, rationality, independence, **enlightenment**[4], and Being Like Al.

2. If you read some of the literature on Critical Thinking, you will have the sense that you are being welcomed into a new religion. All pains and problems will be **vanquished**[5] by this new and unique faith called Critical Thinking. In truth, that is a fairly accurate description of this highly popular and much promoted **pedagogy**[6].

3. Now, let's start looking at Critical Thinking as if we, in fact, are critical thinkers.

4. The first thing that would need to be stated is that Critical Thinking, after all is said and done, is merely **endorsing**[7] the age-old values of being open-minded and willing to consider all the evidence. Pretty much, that's it.

5. But nobody **disputes**[8] those virtues. So, what are all the high-level educators going on about? What is all this **hype**[9] and **hoopla**[10]? When supposedly smart, enlightened people carry on as if they are **tipsy**[11] on something, you should be on guard. Real critical thinking would **dictate**[12] that, wouldn't it?

6. Critical Thinking basically says to be suspicious of everything, except the fad known as Critical Thinking. It is perhaps best understood as a new and **watered-down**[13] version of an earlier fad called **Deconstruction**[14]. That was just a fancy word for **debunking**[15]. Basically, Deconstruction told college students to **dismantle**[16] everything, everything except Deconstruction.

7. Yes, that's what we've got here, another oh-so-clever and highly

selective way to encourage students to épatez les bourgeoisie and to tell Mom and Dad to take a hike.

8. After you **strip**[17] away all the high-minded **rhetoric**[18], Critical Thinking is typically used to tell students that they should not trust conventional wisdom, tradition, religion, parents, and all that irrelevant, old-fashioned stuff.

9. Critical Thinking, somewhat surprisingly, also turns out to be highly **contemptuous**[19] of facts and knowledge. The **formulation**[20] in public schools goes like this: children must learn how to think, not what to think. WHAT is, of course, all the academic content and **scholarly**[21] knowledge that schools used to teach.

10. Now you may be having a **glimmer**[22] of where this thing leads. "What" is out, excluded, **delegitimized**[23]. Students exist in a **perpetual**[24] state of "how". They **evaluate**[25] information, they **juggle**[26] information, they do just about every imaginable thing with information except know it, that is, make it their own.

11. Critical Thinking is very clear on this matter. Most facts are **obsolete**[27]; they are in a state of **flux**[28], or they are readily available on the Internet. It all adds up to the same thing: students need not bother knowing any facts. You discuss them. You don't know them.

12. To the Education Establishment, knowledge is the **perennial**[29] enemy for almost a century. To fight it, our top educators come up with one **sophistry**[30] after another. Critical Thinking is the latest and perhaps slickest. Who will dare to say they are against Critical Thinking?

13. Critical Thinking, we are told, is mankind's highest activity. Critical Thinkers, it's repeated again and again, are a new and higher breed. They exist in a **rarefied**[31], perpetual state of HOW. They don't bother with WHAT.

14. The problem is, basic facts such as "Paris is the capital of France" are neither obsolete nor in the process of change. They are old reliables and need to be **acquired**[32]. Facts are things you have in your head so you can discuss the evening news, European politics, or history. Critical Thinking says hell no to all that.

15. Critical Thinking is another of those alleged breakthroughs to enlightenment that sweep through our schools every few years. Textbooks must be thrown out, teachers must forget what they know, education

schools must be **revamped**[33], and classrooms must be rearranged and restructured. Everything starts over in Year Zero, and everyone must serve the all-**devouring**[34] needs of Critical Thinking. First step: don't bother teaching anything.

16. Critical Thinking, which claims to increase a child's intellectual **sophistication**[35], is actually used to keep the child in a state of perpetual ignorance and shallowness. They play with knowledge. They don't master it or acquire it.

17. Let's take the simplest examples. You want to learn to play the piano, to fly a plane, or to be a bartender. In every case, you have to start acquiring the facts and skills that go with these jobs. You can't sit around talking about the job in some abstract realm, or discussing how it must feel to be a pianist or a bartender.

18. The point is, you have to get your hands dirty in the actual knowledge of the world, of the field, of the discipline. It's only when you know a lot of basic information that you could actually engage in genuine critical thinking.

19. Take something as complex as a war or as simple as a poem. It's only when you know lots of specifics about several wars or a group of poems that you can start making smart comments. You can compare and contrast. You can rank. You can play armchair general or be a literary critic. At this point you are actually engaged in real critical thinking. But Critical Thinking **forecloses**[36] this possibility because students are told not to learn the basic facts.

20. Do you think I exaggerate? Consider what a school teacher wrote of his experiences in California's public schools:

21. "It seemed that memorization of the times tables damaged a child's ability to do critical thinking in math, that, for older kids, concepts like measuring one's distance from a celestial object using parallax should never be taught, rather children should 'discover' or 'construct' it for themselves (an approach called 'constructivism'), again to preserve 'critical thinking skills'."

22. "I was directed in no uncertain terms to immediately cease all instruction in phonics, spelling and grammar, as these would—you guessed it—destroy all hope of reading with critical thinking skills."

23. That's what I meant by the all-devouring needs of Critical Thinking.

Note that anything the child actually learns or knows will get in the way of the true goal, Critical Thinking. Students must essentially be ignorant **primitives**[37], as they struggle to reinvent language and math for themselves. (Here you see that Critical Thinking **aligns**[38] perfectly with the other big fad, **Constructivism**[39].)

24. Here's some **puffery**[40] from a site devoted to the techniques of Critical Thinking:

25. "Socrates established the fact that one cannot depend upon those in 'authority' to have sound knowledge and insight. He demonstrated that persons may have power and high position and yet be deeply confused and **irrational**[41]. He established the importance of asking deep questions that **probe**[42] profoundly into thinking before we accept ideas as worthy of belief."

26. For me, that's priceless. These poor **sophists**[43], unable to think critically, don't see that their **pretext**[44] for Critical Thinking should first be applied to themselves. Are they not persons with power and high position who may well be deeply confused and irrational? Have they really asked the deeper questions and probed profoundly?

27. No. That's why they keep coming up with cynical education ideas that **sabotage**[45] education.

28. Sure, I'm prejudiced. But I suspect this essay is a better example of critical thinking than Critical Thinking is.

29. You don't need to be a weatherman to know which way the wind blows. The Education Establishment wants to create content-light, always politically correct, almost fact-free schools. Then they'll **jury-rig**[46] "alternative assessment techniques" that give nearly every student a high grade. They'll do that with big, impressive-sounding but ultimately not very **substantial**[47] "projects". Parents will be told that their children are learning the "critical thinking skills" vital for "success in the 21st century". For example, what should students do if they see pollution in a nearby lake? Report it to the proper authorities. Use the Internet to find out more about the factory on this lake. Start a pollution awareness campaign. Support the Green candidate in the next election. That's good "critical thinking", so the students get an A, which is not to say the students are educated.

30. The greatest enemy of real critical thinking has not been mentioned. Our public schools have **embraced**[48] an **ethos**[49] of imprecision. Close answers

count. Sometimes correct answers don't count (students are graded on explaining the process). In many situations, students are encouraged to guess. Correct grammar and spelling are not considered important. Throughout the system, under one pretext or another, FUZZINESS is the name of the game. Fuzzy anything is the opposite of critical anything. That the same people who accept all this fuzziness would turn around and embrace **genuine**[50] critical thinking seems unlikely.

(From Bruce Dietrick Price's "Critical Thinking: Not All That Critical")

Vocabulary

1. **snarl** /snɑːl/

v. say in a fierce, angry way 厉声说；吼叫着说

2. **synonymous** /sɪˈnɒnɪməs/

adj. very closely associated with each other so that one suggests the other or one cannot exist without the other (与……)关系紧密的；等同(于)……的

e.g. Paris has always been synonymous with elegance, luxury and style.

3. **impartiality** /ɪmˌpɑːʃɪˈæləti/

n. the state of not being directly involved in a particular situation, and therefore able to give a fair opinion or decision about it 不偏不倚；公正

4. **enlightenment** /ɪnˈlaɪtnmənt/

n. the act of enlightening or the state of being enlightened 启发；启蒙

5. **vanquish** /ˈvæŋkwɪʃ/

v. defeat completely in a battle or a competition (彻底)征服；击败

e.g. At first she shivered from her fear but at last she could vanquish it.

6. **pedagogy** /ˈpedəgɒdʒi/

n. the study and theory of the methods and principles of teaching 教育学；教学法

7. **endorse** /ɪnˈdɔːs/

v. say publicly that you support or approve (公开地)赞同；支持

e.g. I can endorse their opinion wholeheartedly.

8. **dispute** /dɪˈspjuːt/

v. say that it is incorrect or untrue 质疑；对……表示异议

e.g. He disputed the allegations that the infectious disease was spread by some scientists intentionally.

9. hype /haɪp/

n. the use of a lot of publicity and advertising to make people interested in something such as a product 天花乱坠的广告宣传；炒作

e.g. My products aren't based on advertising hype. They sell by word of mouth.

10. hoopla /ˈhuːplɑː/

n. blatant or sensational promotion 大吹大擂；噱头

11. tipsy /ˈtɪpsi/

adj. very drunk 喝醉的；醉醺醺的

12. dictate /dɪkˈteɪt/

v. issue commands or orders 命令

e.g. Commonsense now dictates that it would be wise to sell a few shares.

13. water down

make ... much weaker and less forceful, or less likely to make people angry 使打折扣；削弱

e.g. We have to water down the curriculum for the slow learning class.

14. deconstruction /ˌdiːkənˈstrʌkʃn/

n. a philosophical theory of criticism (usually of literature or film) that seeks to expose deep-seated contradictions in a work by delving below its surface meaning 解构；拆析

15. debunk /ˌdiːˈbʌŋk/

v. show that it is false or not as good as people think it is 指出……的错误；揭穿……的吹嘘（或虚假）

e.g. For more than 50 years, scientists and dog lovers have been trying to debunk the dog-years myth.

16. dismantle /dɪsˈmæntl/

v. cause it to stop functioning by gradually reducing its power or purpose (逐渐)废除；撤销

e.g. Koplan was more blunt, calling it a waste of money to develop a program that works and then dismantle it.

17. strip /strɪp/

v. remove everything that covers it 除去；剥去

e.g. He was disgraced and stripped of his title.

18. rhetoric /ˈretərɪk/

n. not sincere or honest words 花言巧语；华丽的词藻；浮夸之词

e.g. He is stronger on rhetoric than on concrete action.

19. contemptuous /kənˈtemptʃuəs/

adj. showing dislike or disrespect 蔑视的；藐视的；鄙视的

e.g. He was contemptuous of poor people.

20. formulation /ˌfɔːmjuˈleɪʃn/

n. a substance prepared according to a formula; the way in which you express your thoughts and ideas 配方；(想法的)阐述方式；表达方法

21. scholarly /ˈskɒləli/

adj. containing a lot of academic information and is intended for academic readers (书籍、文章)学术的；学术性的

22. glimmer /ˈɡlɪmə(r)/

n. a very slight feeling or look that is not easily noticed 微弱的迹象

e. g. Their first meeting with the new boss gave them a glimmer of what they could expect.

23. delegitimize /ˌdiːlɪˈdʒɪtɪmaɪz/

v. make it illegal 取消合法地位

e. g. After the disaster caused by Nazism, one of the priorities was to delegitimize the ideology of the inequality of races.

24. perpetual /pəˈpetʃuəl/

adj. happening again and again, which seems never to end 连续不断的；无尽无休的

e. g. His mind is in a state of perpetual restlessness, thinking how the sick person may be cured.

25. evaluate /ɪˈvæljueɪt/

v. consider in order to make a judgment 评估；评价

e. g. The market situation is difficult to evaluate.

26. juggle /ˈdʒʌɡl/

v. organize information, figures, money, etc. in the most useful and effective way 有效组织、利用(信息、数字、金钱等)

e. g. The management team meets several times a week to juggle budgets and resources.

27. obsolete /ˈɒbsəliːt/

adj. no longer needed because something better has been invented 过时的；淘汰的

e. g. So much equipment becomes obsolete almost as soon as it's made.

28. flux /flʌks/

n. constant change 变动；流动

e. g. Our society is in a state of flux.

29. perennial /pəˈreniəl/

adj. keeping occurring or seeming to exist all the time 永恒的；持续的；亘古不变的

e. g. There's a perennial shortage of teachers with science qualifications.

30. sophistry /ˈsɒfɪstri/

n. the practice of using clever arguments that sound convincing but are in fact false 诡辩

e.g. Political selection is more dependent on sophistry and less on economic literacy.

31. rarefy /ˈreərɪfaɪ/

v. lessen the density or solidity of 使稀少；使纯化

32. acquire /əˈkwaɪə(r)/

v. learn or develop 获得（技能）；养成（习惯）

e.g. I've never acquired a taste for wine.

33. revamp /ˌriːˈvæmp/

v. make changes in order to try and improve 修补；修改；改进

e.g. They are revamping the old house.

34. devour /dɪˈvaʊə(r)/

v. eat quickly and eagerly 狼吞虎咽地吃；吞食

e.g. She devoured half an apple pie.

35. sophistication /səˌfɪstɪˈkeɪʃn/

n. the quality of being intelligent and knowing a lot 精明老练

36. foreclose /fɔːˈkləʊz/

v. keep from happening or arising; have the effect of preventing 阻止

e.g. They tried to foreclose the possibility of his meeting with the press.

37. primitive /ˈprɪmətɪv/

n. a person who belongs to early stage of civilization 原始人

38. align /əˈlaɪn/

v. support because having the same political aim 与……联合；与……结盟

e.g. There are signs that the prime minister is aligning himself with the liberals.

39. constructivism /kənˈstrʌktɪvɪzəm/

n. a theory which stresses construction in learning 建构主义

40. puffery /ˈpʌfəri/

n. too much praise 吹捧

e.g. Using puffery to raise awareness of products is illegal.

41. irrational /ɪˈræʃənl/

adj. not based on logical reasons or clear thinking 不合逻辑的；不合理的；荒谬的

e.g. My subconscious self is expressing irrational fears.

42. probe /prəʊb/

v. ask questions or try to discover facts about something 调查；打探

e.g. The policeman made efforts to probe into the case of murder.

43. sophist /ˈsɒfɪst/

n. a deceptive person who offers clever-sounding but flawed arguments or explanations 诡辩家；诡辩者

44. pretext /ˈpriːtekst/

n. a reason which somebody gives to do something 借口；托词

e. g. He excused himself on the pretext of a stomach upset.

45. sabotage /ˈsæbətɑːʒ/

v. destroy property or hinder normal operations or deliberately prevent it from being successful 阻挠；妨碍；暗中破坏

e. g. My ex-wife deliberately sabotages my access to the children.

46. jury-rig /ˈdʒʊriˌrɪg/

v. do or use whatever is available 临时或应急配备

47. substantial /səbˈstænʃl/

adj. large in amount or degree; actual, true, not imaginary; solid, strong, firm 大量的；相当程度的；重大的；真实的；实质的

e. g. Substantial numbers of people support the plan.

There's a substantial difference of opinion within the group.

48. embrace /ɪmˈbreɪs/

v. accept something and start supporting it or believing in it 欣然接受；支持

e. g. He embraces the new information age.

49. ethos /ˈiːθɒs/

n. the set of ideas and attitudes that is associated with a particular group of people or a particular type of activity 气质；精神特质；风气；思潮

e. g. The whole ethos of the hotel is effortless service.

50. genuine /ˈdʒenjuɪn/

adj. not false or of an imitation 真正的；非伪造的；名副其实的

e. g. Is the painting a genuine Picasso?

Exercises for Text 1

I. Read the text and answer the questions.

1. What do many people think of critical thinking?
2. What is critical thinking in essence in the author's view?
3. What's the author's criticism of the way of teaching critical thinking?
4. How should we treat facts in school education?
5. What are the implications of this article for Chinese education?

>>> Unit 1 Critical Thinking

II. Complete the sentences with the words below. Change the form where necessary.

contemptuous	dispute	dismantle	glimmer	evaluate
hype	acquire	synonymous	align	substantial
revamp	sabotage	endorse	devour	embrace
flux	vanquish	perpetual	probe	pretext

1. With knowledge and wisdom, evil could be _____ on this earth.
2. The construction of the road was deliberately _____ by the terrorists and wouldn't be finished on time.
3. We all agree that it is time to _____ the system in the factory so that it will be better.
4. We are certainly seeing a lot of _____ by some companies which turns out to be exaggeration.
5. Going grey is not necessarily _____ with growing old. Some young people also have grey hair.
6. All of these secondary schools did not _____ Progressive Education practices, however. Some schools are even strongly against the practices.
7. Nobody _____ that Davey was clever, but he did make a lot of mistakes.
8. Chris _____ the bike in five minutes, but then he found that he couldn't fix it.
9. He's openly _____ of all the major competitors and thinks of them as having no ability.
10. Despite an occasional _____ of hope, this campaign has not produced any results.
11. I thought her _____ complaints were going to prove too much for me.
12. They will first send in trained nurses to _____ the needs of the individual situation.
13. Education remains in a state of _____ which will take some time to settle down.
14. Having read the book, she will be able to pass on the _____ knowledge to trainee teachers.
15. A medium-sized dog will _____ at least one can of food per day.
16. Domestic prices have been _____ with those in world markets so that they will not be much higher than those in world markets.
17. The more they _____ into his background, the more inflamed their suspicions would become.
18. They wanted a(n) _____ for not allowing their kids to go and at last they found one.

19. That is a very _____ improvement in the present situation, which really encourages people.
20. Mr McCain is certainly the right man for the job, but we are not yet ready to _____ him for the position of manager.

III. Translate the sentences into Chinese.

1. Critical Thinking is typically used to tell students that they should not trust conventional wisdom, tradition, religion, parents, and all that irrelevant, old-fashioned stuff.
2. The formulation in public schools goes like this: children must learn how to think, not what to think.
3. Students exist in a perpetual state of "how". They evaluate information, they juggle information, they do just about every imaginable thing with information except know it, that is, make it their own.
4. Then they'll jury-rig "alternative assessment techniques" that give nearly every student a high grade. They'll do that with big, impressive-sounding but ultimately not very substantial "projects".
5. Throughout the system, under one pretext or another, FUZZINESS is the name of the game.

>>> Unit 1　Critical Thinking

READING & CRITICAL THINKING

Text 2

On Critical Thinking

Johann N. Neem

1. Everywhere we turn these days, we hear that colleges are not teaching "critical thinking". Employers want critical thinkers, but they cannot find them. Entire books conclude that colleges have failed to increase students' critical thinking. Nicholas Lemann, former dean of Columbia's School of Journalism, urges colleges to **foreground**[1] method, not content, in their general education programs. Many **high-profile**[2] reformers agree that professors too often focus on "content" over "skills", thus failing to prepare students to be learners.

2. **Advocates**[3] of critical thinking contrast thinking critically with learning knowledge. College professors, they proclaim, teach a bunch of stuff (facts, dates, formulae) that students don't need and won't use. Instead, students need to have intellectual and **cognitive**[4] skills. As *New York Times* columnist Thomas Friedman has **proclaimed**[5], "the world doesn't care anymore what you know but what you can do".

3. There are two problems with this **perspective**[6]. First, it is fundamentally anti-intellectual. It presumes that the material colleges teach—the arts and sciences—does not matter, when, in fact, this is the very reason colleges exist. Second, these claims are wrong. Cognitive science demonstrates that if we want critical thinkers, we need to ensure that they have knowledge. Thinking cannot be separated from knowledge. Instead, critical thinking is learning to use our knowledge. The most effective critical thinkers, then, are those who learn history or physics. The stuff we learn about matters.

4. In many ways, the turn to skills is a defensive response. At a time when the humanities, in particular, are under attack, what better way to defend the **humanities**[7] "useless knowledge" than by demonstrating that

these are means to a larger end: critical thinking? However, one must acknowledge that these defenses reflect the **capitulation**[8] of academics to **utilitarian**[9] and **pragmatic**[10] pressures. Lacking a convincing argument for the knowledge that **anthropologists**[11] or historians have to offer, they instead proclaim that history and anthropology will serve employers' needs better than will other fields. But if that's the case, why does one really need to know anything about anthropology or history? Why should colleges hire anthropologists or historians instead of professors of critical thinking?

5. This is not an abstract question. When we turn from higher education to the K-12 system, we see that the focus on skills over knowledge has transformed the curriculum. Increasingly, especially under the Common Core State Standards, students devote their energies to learning skills, but they may not learn as much history or civics or science. Therefore, in contrast to the anti-intellectual rhetoric of many reformers, critical thinking must be defended because it encourages students to gain more insight from the arts and sciences.

6. Imagine your employer provided you with a **manual**[12] **dexterity**[13] class in which you learned to move your fingers about effectively. Now imagine that you came to a guitar teacher and asked for credit. Certainly, guitar players need to have manual dexterity, but the guitar teacher would wonder why you deserved credit. Learning dexterity absent actually playing guitar is not particularly valuable. It certainly does not mean that one can play guitar, nor that one has understood guitar or embraced the purpose of studying guitar. It's a meaningless skill from the perspective of a guitar teacher. The same is true about critical thinking in the arts and sciences. Critical thinking is not enough and on its own, isolated from meaningful subject matter, is unimportant.

7. How, then, should colleges and universities understand skills? They should see them in relation to the goods of liberal education. This means that skills should be developed in the context of reading and writing about literature or history or engaging in scientific inquiry. **Collegians**[14] care about the question, "Critical thinking to what end?" Colleges' goal should be to encourage students and professors to gain as much insight from studying history or economics or physics or chemistry as possible. In other words, critical thinking is not a self-standing goal independent of the larger purpose of a college education; instead, it should be intimately connected to developing students' intellectual virtues, habits, and knowledge.

8. What do we mean by critical thinking? Often, advocates of critical thinking portray it as an independent set of cognitive skills that are easily transferable. They advocate critical thinkers because employers and political leaders want people who can solve complex problems, but they do not care much about what students think about. Colleges do. As one **skeptic**[15] of "critical thinking" has written, "If we describe college courses mainly as delivery mechanisms for skills to please a future employer, if we imply that history, literature, and linguistics are more or less interchangeable 'content' that convey the same mental tools, we oversimplify the intellectual complexity that makes a university education worthwhile in the first place."

9. At a deeper, more profound level, critical thinking can be seen as a disciplined activity on its own terms. Indeed, one might understand it as a **revival**[16] of the **trivium**[17] of grammar, rhetoric, and logic. These were the original liberal arts, and the term "arts" meant techniques to analyze texts and problems. In this sense, critical thinking can be understood as a deep activity, one that requires the development of new habits of mind. It is not something we can get without extensive study and practice. The skills that we apply to problems and texts, the capacity to understand arguments, to make sense of their strengths and weaknesses, and to offer new and creative solutions is gained by consistent and constant study over years.

10. Yet even this more profound understanding of critical thinking cannot be separated from learning subject matter in the arts and sciences. We can only think critically about things about which we have knowledge, and we can only make use of facts if we know how to think about them. As James Lang writes in *Small Teaching: Everyday Lessons from the Science of Learning*, "Knowledge is foundational: we won't have the structures in place to do deep thinking if we haven't spent time mastering a body of knowledge related to that thinking." For example, the answer one might expect to the question "Why do we have global warming?" would be very different from a student with background knowledge in chemistry or public policy or economics than from someone who had not studied these subjects. An ignorant person may well conclude, in a great demonstration of "critical thinking", that the earth is getting warmer because the sun is getting hotter. It makes sense, it's reasonable, and it is also wrong. The same is true for almost any sophisticated question.

11. This happens. When students graduating from Harvard College and ninth graders at Cambridge Rindge and Latin School were asked about the seasons, they demonstrated amazing levels of "critical thinking", but they did not have the background knowledge to get the correct answer. Many believed that the seasons were caused by the Earth's orbit. Some offered complicated responses that exhibited the students' "critical thinking" and creativity. But they were wrong.

12. One has to know things to answer things. This is true even in the age of Google. If one looks up something online, one needs to know a lot of background information to make sense of the definition and explanation—and given how unreliable many online sources are, without that background knowledge, one might be led **astray**[18]. But perhaps most surprising, those with more knowledge can learn more when they look something up on Google. That's because if they already have background knowledge, they can add to it the new information and insights from what they are learning.

13. In other words, intellectual skills and knowledge are not two **distinct**[19] things. They must work together to produce critical thinkers. Put more **baldly**[20], despite all the rhetoric, there is **no such thing as**[21] critical thinking in general. People think critically when they know how to use knowledge to solve problems and to generate new knowledge.

(From Johann N. Neem's "What's the Point of College?")

Vocabulary

1. foreground /ˈfɔːɡraʊnd/

v. make something the most important part of a description or account 强调;使突出

e.g. His book foregrounds the importance of drawing conclusion by doing experiments.

2. high-profile /ˌhaɪˈprəʊfaɪl/

adj. receiving or involving a lot of attention and discussion on television, in newspapers, etc. 高调的;备受关注的

3. **advocate** /ˈædvəkeɪt/

n. someone who recommends something publicly 拥护者；提倡者

e. g. He was a strong advocate of those policies.

4. **cognitive** /ˈkɒɡnətɪv/

adj. relating to the mental process involved in knowing, learning, and understanding things 认识过程的；认知的

e. g. Vygotsky's theory of cognitive development is very convincing.

5. **proclaim** /prəˈkleɪm/

v. state it in an emphatic way 明确表示；清楚地表明

e. g. "I think we have been heard today," he proclaimed.

6. **perspective** /pəˈspektɪv/

n. particular way of thinking about something, especially one that is influenced by one's beliefs or experiences(尤指受到某种思想、经验影响的)思考方法；态度；观点；角度

e. g. He says the death of his father 18 months ago has given him a new perspective on life.

7. **humanities** /hjuːˈmænɪtɪz/

n. subjects such as history, philosophy, and literature which are concerned with human ideas and behaviour(历史、哲学、文学等)人文学科

8. **capitulation** /kəˌpɪtʃuˈleɪʃn/

n. the act of surrendering (under agreed conditions) 屈服

9. **utilitarian** /ˌjuːtɪlɪˈteəriən/

adj. based on the idea that the morally correct course of action is the one that produces benefit for the greatest number of people 功利主义的；实利主义的

e. g. James Mill was famous for his utilitarian ideas.

10. **pragmatic** /præɡˈmætɪk/

adj. based on practical considerations, rather than theoretical ones 讲求实效的；实用的；务实的；讲求实际的

e. g. A pragmatic approach to the problems is faced by Latin America. They can solve the problems soon.

11. **anthropologist** /ˌænθrəˈpɒlədʒɪst/

n. a social scientist who specializes in anthropology 人类学家

12. **manual** /ˈmænjuəl/

adj. made by someone's hands 用手的；手工的

13. **dexterity** /dekˈsterəti/

n. skill in using hands or mind(双手的)灵巧；(思维的)敏捷

14. **collegian** /kəˈliːdʒən/

n. a student (or former student) at a college or university 大学生；大学毕业生

15. skeptic /ˈskeptɪk/

n. someone who habitually doubts accepted beliefs 怀疑论者

16. revival /rɪˈvaɪvl/

n. the process of becoming active or popular again 复苏；复兴；恢复；再次流行

e.g. This return to realism has produced a revival of interest in a number of artists.

17. trivium /ˈtrɪviəm/

n. grammar, logic and rhetoric（中世纪大学的）三学科

18. astray /əˈstreɪ/

adj. making somebody believe something which is not true, causing somebody to make a wrong decision 误导的；使做错误决定的

e.g. Jack's parents thought the other boys might lead him astray.

19. distinct /dɪˈstɪŋkt/

adj. different or separate from 有区别的；不同的；个别的

e.g. This book is divided into two distinct parts.

20. baldly /ˈbɔːldli/

adv. frankly 坦率地

21. no such thing as 没有像……这样的事

e.g. There's no such thing as absolute morality.

Exercises for Text 2

I. Decide whether the statements are true (T) or false (F) according to the text.

1. Supporters of critical thinking think that colleges teach intellectual skills that students need.
2. It is a good way to defend humanities by demonstrating that they are useful to critical thinking.
3. Critical thinking should be supported because it encourages students to get a lot from the study of arts and science.
4. We can't get critical thinking without extensive study and practice.
5. Intellectual skills and knowledge are totally different things.

II. Translate the following sentences with the key words in the parentheses.

1. 他信心百倍地声称他的产品是市场上最物有所值的。(proclaim)
2. 至少到明年8月之前,新车销量回升的希望都微乎其微。(revival)
3. 这部戏剧凸显了父女之间的关系。(foreground)
4. 孩子们成长以后,他们的认知过程变得更加敏锐。(cognitive)
5. 要宽容地接受各种角度的看法。(perspective)

6. 罗宾从实际的角度考虑了一下她的处境。(pragmatic)
7. 我驱车向东去纽约,但地图指错了方向。(astray)
8. 工程学和工艺学互不相同。(distinct)
9. 坦白说,如果你不戒烟,这病就治不好。(baldly)
10. 世上哪有不付钱白吃的好事。(no such thing as)

III. Explain the following sentences in your own words.

1. Learning dexterity absent actually playing guitar is not particularly valuable.
2. At a time when the humanities, in particular, are under attack, what better way to defend the humanities "useless knowledge" than by demonstrating that these are means to a larger end: critical thinking?
3. That's because if they already have background knowledge, they can add to it the new information and insights from what they are learning.
4. Colleges' goal should be to encourage students and professors to gain as much insight from studying history or economics or physics or chemistry as possible.
5. In this sense, critical thinking can be understood as a deep activity, one that requires the development of new habits of mind.

Learning Strategies

Understanding Difficult Sentences by Analyzing the Structure

When we read the original works of educators, we often come across many difficult sentences which might frighten us into giving up reading. When this happens, don't panic and surrender. We can pause and analyze the structure of those sentences. After analyzing the structure, we will find we actually understand the sentence!

For example, "That the same people who accept all this fuzziness would turn around and embrace genuine critical thinking seems unlikely." The basic structure of this sentence is "that ... seems unlikely". The long subject clause serves as the subject and "seems unlikely" serves as the predicate. When you are clear about the structure of this sentence, you also begin to understand it.

Now, it's your turn to figure out the meaning of the following difficult sentences:

1. The skills that we apply to problems and texts, the capacity to understand arguments, to make sense of their strengths and weaknesses, and to offer new and creative solutions is gained by consistent and constant study over years.
2. For example, the answer one might expect to the question "Why do we have global warming?" would be very different from a student with background

knowledge in chemistry or public policy or economics than from someone who had not studied these subjects.
3. It's only when you know lots of specifics about several wars or a group of poems that you can start making smart comments.

Unit Project

Lots of Chinese scholars strongly criticize Chinese students' lack of critical thinking ability. Some worry that those who receive primary school, middle school and college education in China will not be able to think critically. They deem Western education as the best solution and call on Chinese teachers to follow the example of Western schools. Work in groups to make research on articles criticizing Chinese students' lack of critical thinking ability and make a presentation about it for 10 minutes.

1. Find articles criticizing Chinese students' lack of critical thinking ability and sum up their views.
2. Hold a discussion in groups about whether you agree with the views of those articles.
3. Give an analysis of those articles by using the two writers' views.
4. Make a presentation about it for 10 minutes to your classmates.

>>> Unit 2 Liberal Arts

Unit 2

Liberal Arts

Pre-reading questions:

1. What do you know about liberal arts education?
2. Why do lots of educators think liberal arts education is very important?

Text 1

Who Killed the Liberal Arts?

Joseph Epstein

1. When asked what he thought about the cultural wars, Irving Kristol is said to have replied, "They're over," adding, "We lost." If Kristol was correct, one of the decisive battles in that war may have been over the liberal arts in education, which we also lost. In a loose definition, the "liberal arts" denote college study anchored in **preponderantly**[1] Western literature, philosophy, and history, with science, mathematics, and foreign languages playing a substantial, though less central role; in more recent times, the social science subjects—psychology, sociology, political science—have also sometimes been included. The liberal arts have always been distinguished from more specialized, usually vocational training. For the ancient Greeks, the liberal arts were the subjects thought necessary for a free man to study. If he is to remain free, in this view, he must acquire knowledge of the best thought of the past, which will cultivate in him the intellectual depth and critical spirit required to live in an informed and reasonable way in the present.

2. For many years, the liberal arts were my second religion. I worshipped their content, I believed in their significance, I fought for them against the philistines of our age as Samson fought against the **Philistines**[2] of his—though in my case, I kept my hair and brought down no pillars. As currently practiced, however, it is becoming more and more difficult to defend the liberal arts. Their content has been **drastically**[3] changed, their significance is in doubt, and defending them in the condition in which they linger on scarcely seems worth the struggle.

3. The loss of prestige of the liberal arts is part of the general crisis of higher education in the United States. The crisis begins in economics. Larger numbers of Americans start college, but roughly a third never finish—more women finish, interestingly, than do men. With the economic **slump**[4] of recent

>>> Unit 2　Liberal Arts

years, **benefactions**[5] to colleges are down, as are federal and state grants, thus forcing tuition costs up, in public as well as in private institutions. Inflation is greater in the **realm**[6] of higher education than in any other public sphere. Complaints about the high cost of education at private colleges—fees of $50,000 and $55,000 a year are commonly mentioned—are heard everywhere. A great number of students leave college with enormous student-loan debt, which is higher than either national credit card or automobile credit debt. Because of the expense of traditional liberal arts colleges, greater numbers of the young go to one or another form of commuter college, usually for vocational training.

　　4. Although it is common knowledge that a person with a college degree will earn a great deal more than a person without one—roughly a million dollars more over a lifetime is the frequently cited figure—today, students with college degrees are finding it tough to get decent jobs. People are beginning to wonder if college, at its currently extravagant price, is worth it. Is higher education, like tech stocks and real estate, the next big bubble to burst? A great deal of evidence for the crisis in American higher education is set out in *College: What It Was, Is, and Should Be*. Its author, Andrew Delbanco, the biographer of Herman Melville, is a **staunch**[7] defender of liberal arts, as he himself studied them as an undergraduate at Harvard and as he teaches them currently at Columbia. The continuing **diminution**[8] of the liberal arts worries him. Some 18 million people in the United States are now enrolled in one or another kind of undergraduate institution of higher learning—but fewer than 100,000 are enrolled in liberal arts colleges.

　　5. At the same time, for that small number of elite liberal arts colleges—Harvard, Yale, Princeton, Stanford, Duke, the University of Chicago, and a few others—applications continue to rise, despite higher and higher tuition fees. The **ardor**[9] to get into these schools—for economic, social, and **snobbish**[10] reasons—has brought about an examination culture, at least among the children of the well-to-do, who from preschool on are **relentlessly**[11] trained to take the examinations that will get them into the better grade schools, high schools, colleges, and, finally, professional schools. Professor Delbanco is opposed to the economic unfairness behind these arrangements, believing, rightly, that as a result, "the obstacles to getting into the **elite**[12] colleges that bright low-income students face today are more **insidious**[13] than the frank exclusionary practices that once prevailed".

6. Whether students today, despite all their special tutoring and testing, are any better than those of earlier generations is far from clear. Trained almost from the cradle to smash the SATs and any other examination that stands in their way, the privileged among them may take examinations better, but it is doubtful if their learning and intellectual understanding are any greater. Usually propelled by the desires of their parents, they form a **meritocracy**[14] that, in Delbanco's view, as in that of the English sociologist Michael Young whom he quotes, comprises a **dystopia**[15] of sorts, **peopled**[16] by young men and women driven by high, but empty, ambition. "Are these really the people we want running the world?" Delbanco asks. Unfortunately, they already are. I am not the only one, surely, to have noticed that some of the worst people in this country—names on request—are graduates of the Harvard and Yale law schools.

7. Attending one of a limited number of elite colleges continues to yield wide opportunities for graduates, but fewer and fewer people any longer believe that someone who has finished college is necessarily all that much smarter than someone who hasn't. With standards lowered, hours of study shortened, reports appearing about how many college graduates can no longer be depended upon to know how to write or to grasp **rudimentary**[17] intellectual concepts, having gone to college seems to have less and less bearing on a person's intelligence.

8. Studies cited by Delbanco in his footnotes claim an increase among college students in cheating, drinking, and depression. In their book *Academically Adrift*, Richard Arum and Josipa Roska argue that the gain in critical thinking and complex reasoning among the majority of students during college years is very low, if not minimal. In an article in *The **Chronicle***[18] *of Higher Education* drawn from their book, Arum and Roska write:

9. Parents—although somewhat **disgruntled**[19] about increasing costs—want colleges to provide a safe environment where their children can mature, gain independence, and attain a **credential**[20] that will help them be successful as adults. Students in general seek to enjoy the benefits of a full collegiate experience that is focused as much on social life as on academic pursuits, while earning high marks in their courses with relatively little investment of effort. Professors are eager to find time to concentrate on their scholarship

>>> Unit 2　Liberal Arts

and professional interests. Administrators have been asked to focus largely on external institutional rankings and the financial bottom line. Government funding agencies are primarily interested in the development of new scientific knowledge. No actors in the system are primarily interested in undergraduates' academic growth, although many are interested in student retention and persistence.

10. What savvy employers are likely to conclude is that those who graduate from college are probably more **conformist**[21], and therefore likely to be more dependable, than those who do not. Paul Goodman, one of the now-forgotten **gurus**[22] of the 1960s, used to argue that what finishing college really meant is that one was willing to do anything to succeed in a capitalist society. In getting a college degree, Goodman held, one was in effect saying, I want in on the game, deal me a hand, I want desperately to play. Education, meanwhile, didn't have a lot to do with it.

11. Not everywhere in higher education have standards slipped. One assumes that in engineering and within the sciences they have been maintained, and in some ways, owing to computer technology, perhaps improved. Relatively new fields of learning, computer science chief among them, have not been around long enough to have lost their way. Medical and legal education are probably not greatly different than they have traditionally been. Chiefly in the liberal arts subjects do standards seem most radically to have slipped.

12. Early in the 19th century, Sydney Smith, one of the founders of *The Edinburgh Review*, remarked that if we had made the same progress in the **culinary**[23] arts as we have made in education, we should still be eating soup with our hands. Apart from eliminating **corporal punishment**[24] and widening the educational **franchise**[25], we can't be sure if, over the centuries, we have made much progress in education. At the moment there is great enthusiasm about "advances" in education owing to the Internet. Two teachers at Stanford, for example, put their course on Artificial Intelligence online and drew an audience of 160,000 students from all around the world. But science, which deals in one right answer, is more easily taught without a physical presence in the room, and probably works better online than humanities courses, whose questions usually have many answers, few of them permanently right. *The Washington Monthly*, in its May-June issue, has a

special section called "The Next Wave of School Reform", a wave that, in the words of the editor, aims to "improve students' ability to think critically and independently, solve complex problems, apply knowledge to novel situations, work in teams and communicate effectively". The problem with these waves of school reform, of course, is that a new one is always needed because the last one turns out to have tossed up more **detritus**[26] on the shore than was expected.

(From Joseph Epstein's "Who Killed the Liberal Arts?")

Vocabulary

1. preponderantly /prɪˈpɒndərəntli/
adv. much greater in number or influence 占优势地；占多数地
e.g. The patients are preponderantly black.

2. Philistine /ˈfɪlɪstaɪn/
n. 非利士人

3. drastically /ˈdrɑːstɪkli/
adv. completely 彻底地；剧烈地
e.g. The supply of money in circulation was drastically reduced overnight.

4. slump /slʌmp/
1) *n.* a sudden large reduction in amount 急剧下降；暴跌
   e.g. The slump in the financial markets smashed him.
2) *v.* fall suddenly and by a large amount 急剧下降；暴跌
   e.g. Sales have slumped this year. This is going to be a difficult year for many people.

5. benefaction /ˌbenɪˈfækʃn/
n. an act intending or showing kindness and good will 善行；善举；捐赠

6. realm /relm/
n. any area of activity, interest, or thought (活动、兴趣或思想的) 领域；范围
e.g. Students' interests are mostly limited to the academic realm.

7. staunch /stɔːntʃ/
adj. very loyal to a person, organization, or set of beliefs, and supporting them strongly 坚定的；忠诚的；虔诚的

e. g. He's a staunch supporter of controls on unnecessary spending.

8. diminution /ˌdɪmɪˈnjuːʃn/

n. reducing; decreasing 减少;降低

e. g. They tried to prevent the diminution of resources.

9. ardor /ˈɑːdə/

n. passion 狂热;热情

e. g. The students were much impressed by their teacher's ardor in teaching.

10. snobbish /ˈsnɒbɪʃ/

adj. too proud of their social status, intelligence, or taste(对自身社会地位、才智、品位等)过分自傲的;势利的

e. g. I'd expected her to be snobbish but she was warm and friendly.

11. relentlessly /rɪˈlentləsli/

adv. cruelly; without stop 残酷地;无情地;不懈地

e. g. He pursued her relentlessly, refusing to take "no" for an answer.

12. elite /eɪˈliːt, ɪˈliːt/

n. the most powerful, rich, or talented people within a particular group, place, or society 精英;杰出人物

e. g. In these countries, only the elite can afford an education for their children.

13. insidious /ɪnˈsɪdiəs/

adj. unpleasant or dangerous and developing gradually without being noticed 隐伏的;潜在的;不知不觉间加剧的

e. g. The changes are insidious, and will not produce a noticeable effect for 15 to 20 years.

14. meritocracy /ˌmerɪˈtɒkrəsi/

n. a society or social system in which people get status or rewards because of what they achieve, rather than because of their wealth or social status 英才管理(制度);贤能统治(社会)

15. dystopia /dɪsˈtəʊpiə/

n. state in which the condition of life is extremely bad as from deprivation or oppression or terror 敌托邦;糟透的社会

16. people /ˈpiːpl/

v. be the people who exist in a place, situation, or period of time 居住在;把……挤满人

17. rudimentary /ˌruːdɪˈmentri/

adj. basic, and not detailed or developed 初步的

e. g. He had only a rudimentary knowledge of French.

18. chronicle /ˈkrɒnɪkl/

n. history, account, annals, journal, narrative 编年史;历史

19. disgruntled /dɪsˈgrʌntld/

adj. not satisfied; not happy 不满的;不高兴的

e. g. I left feeling disgruntled at the way I'd been treated.

20. credential /krəˈdenʃl/

n. a document attesting to the truth of certain stated facts 证书

21. conformist /kənˈfɔːmɪst/

adj. behaving or thinking like everyone else rather than doing things that are original 循规蹈矩的

e. g. He may have to become more conformist if he is to prosper again.

22. guru /ˈguruː/

n. a person who some people regard as an expert or leader 专家;权威;领袖

e. g. These gurus are being promoted by publishers and hyped in the business press.

23. culinary /ˈkʌlməri/

adj. of kitchen 厨房的

e. g. She was keen to acquire more advanced culinary skills.

24. corporal punishment

physical punishment 体罚

25. franchise /ˈfræntʃaɪz/

n. special rights; the rights of civilians 特权;公民权

26. detritus /dɪˈtraɪtəs/

n. pieces of stone 碎石;残渣

Exercises for Text 1

I. Read the text and answer the questions.

1. What do liberal arts refer to? What are they distinguished from?
2. What is examination culture? What are the reasons for this?
3. What do most students choose to learn in American colleges?
4. What do American students and parents expect from universities?
5. What are the consequences of "killing liberal arts" in college?

II. Complete the sentences with the words below. Change the form where necessary.

ardor	utilitarian	relentlessly	retention	persistence
drastically	realm	snobbish	culinary	disgruntle
slump	diminution	guru	flunk	preponderantly
rudimentary	staunch	elite	curriculum	insidious

1. The _____ in the financial markets smashed him. He lost lots of money.
2. You can see how being good in the interpersonal _____ actually was a direct benefit, even for effectively pursuing a technical task.
3. She displayed great _____ for art and this was the most important reason why she could keep on pursuing her dream even in great difficulty.
4. They were accurate in their prediction that he would change her life _____. They almost couldn't recognize her.
5. There appears a(n) _____ tendency in job hunting of university graduates in the face of severe competition. Many students only want to find jobs that can bring them high salary.
6. They were given only _____ training in the job. No wonder they couldn't do the job very well.
7. Gardiner has pursued _____ high standards in performing classical music.
8. Age brought a gradual _____ of his strength and energy. He felt less and less energetic.
9. He is a(n) _____ supporter of discovery learning and thinks of it as the only way to cultivate students' learning ability.
10. He followed the teachings of his _____ fanatically, which is not very rational because no one is error-free.
11. They had a(n) _____ dislike for their intellectual and social inferiors.
12. Public opinion is influenced by the small group of _____ who control the media.
13. Your son is upset because he _____ a history exam.
14. I have a real problem with _____ of information. I tend to forget the information I get very quickly.
15. They focus on overt discrimination rather than _____ aspects of racism.
16. Cantonese chef would consider it a(n) _____ sin of the highest order to produce a dish that was overcooked or too heavily seasoned.
17. Chandra was determined to become a doctor and kept on trying even after many failures. At last, her _____ paid off.
18. Tea, as Chinese traditional industry, is one of the most _____ agricultural products in Zhejiang Province.
19. The employees were _____ by their bad working conditions. The employers should listen to their complaints.
20. Languages are an essential part of the school _____.

III. Translate the sentences into Chinese.

1. I believed in their significance, I fought for them against the philistines of our age as Samson fought against the Philistines of his—though in my case, I kept

my hair and brought down no pillars.
2. If he is to remain free, in this view, he must acquire knowledge of the best thought of the past, which will cultivate in him the intellectual depth and critical spirit required to live in an informed and reasonable way in the present.
3. The obstacles to getting into the elite colleges that bright low-income students face today are more insidious than the frank exclusionary practices that once prevailed.
4. Students in general seek to enjoy the benefits of a full collegiate experience that is focused as much on social life as on academic pursuits, while earning high marks in their courses with relatively little investment of effort.
5. At the moment there is great enthusiasm about "advances" in education owing to the Internet.

> Unit 2   Liberal Arts

READING & CRITICAL THINKING

Text 2
The Danger of a Liberal Arts Education?

Ryan McIlhenny

1. The number of essays **extolling**[1] the importance of a liberal arts education has grown over the last few years. Writers argue that the skills acquired through such an education cultivate within students an ability to provide **innovative**[2] solutions to challenges in the workplace. These well-trained individuals think outside the textbook, so to speak, and beyond the narrow confines of a specific major. Because of such critical-thinking skills, liberal arts graduates are highly valuable—especially to those in the corporate world. Yet there is something that most of these **laudatory**[3] pieces **overlook**[4]: the threat that such an education poses to established power, including corporate power. The liberal arts provide students the theoretical and practical tools needed to contribute to making the world a better place, which often begins by uncovering and confronting abuses of power. For this reason, these writers may need to rethink what exactly they value so highly.

2. Skills-oriented learning of the type provided by a liberal education has the potential to undermine one of the promises made by pie-in-the-sky **proponents**[5] of the liberal arts: to create a generation of leaders. Learning how to become a stand-alone world changer is a common **trope**[6] in the marketing campaigns of consumer-driven institutions. While truth is rarely the objective of such **manipulative**[7] advertising, assume for a moment that schools are in fact able to deliver on their promise, to **churn out**[8] a **plethora**[9] of leaders. These marketing claims immediately face a twofold problem. First, the claims collapse under the weight of their own **contradiction**[10]. Packing the market with leaders would create a leadership **deficit**[11]. By definition, leaders form an elite group. Second, there is often very little explication, during the period between a student's **matriculation**[12] and graduation, of what constitutes a leader.

3. A leader, we might say, is someone who **rallies**[13] and organizes others for the end goal of doing what's right, to **initiate**[14] direct action for the well-being of society. But those in power, including leaders, are not always interested in doing what is right. The sad reality is that many, particularly those under the influence of corporate power, rarely support leaders who seek the betterment of the world, since it can threaten their power. Would those at the top, for instance, really celebrate a liberal arts student who creatively exposes the unethical activities of a multinational corporation? Would a young student at a college or university run by corporate-minded administrators be considered a leader for trying to get at the truth—for example, through activism or articles in the campus newspaper criticizing the administration—despite the efforts of management to shut such a person up? Would they **heed**[15] the critical and creative **insights**[16] of an individual who confronts systems of oppression? The meaning of leadership today is quite restricted. It means, all too often, abiding by the dictates of the corporate world.

4. Many institutions have forgotten the **telos**[17] of a liberal arts education: to train students not how to be but how to become. The word "liberal" in liberal arts comes from "liber", meaning "free" or "to be free". What has been lost in education is the belief that one must work to acquire that freedom. Too many educators simply hand students good grades or are pressured to do so by students themselves or **dictatorial**[18] administrators. Contemporary educators face the overwhelming—and seemingly unstoppable—tidal wave of grade inflation. In many institutions, students receive As with minimal effort (sometimes from instructors who **expend**[19] little effort). Freedom, however, must be worked for and, when achieved, maintained. The "arts" in liberal arts refer to the skills a student needs to reach that freedom. The question that one may ask is "What do we mean by freedom?" It is a freedom that is both from and to—freedom from our individual ignorance and from systems of power that benefit from ignorance as well as the freedom to pursue truth. Education makes powerful agents—agents dedicated to the preservation of truth.

5. In my lower-division US History course, students read *Frederick Douglass's Narrative*, the story of Douglass's life as a slave and his successful journey to freedom. The key skill utilized by Douglass to attain his freedom was learning how to read—a dangerous skill in **antebellum**[20] America. In

many southern states at the time, teaching a slave how to read was banned by law. Why? Slave owners knew exactly the answer to that question. Literacy, Douglass's owner said, "would forever unfit Douglass to be a slave. He would at once become unmanageable, and of no value to his master." Literacy would threaten the power that whites held over blacks. Douglass understood that the important skills of reading and writing could serve as "the pathway from slavery to freedom". Literacy gave Douglas the ability not simply to understand himself (his status as a slave) and the world around him (the evils of slavery), but also to **transform**[21] himself and his world.

6. Again, the idea here is that the liberal arts offer the freedom to be, to act, to contribute to the flourishing of self and world. In order to get to that point, students need to harness their own critical and creative skills. The *critical* begins with reading, seeing, and listening to our life situations. Reading, a skill in which many are **woefully**[22] deficient these days, requires more than understanding the "letter". Higher-level reading enables us to make more intricate connections so that we develop a deeper understanding of reality and, ideally, incorporate into our own lives the life-enhancing words and deeds of those we study, the heroes of the past whom we make relevant to the present. It also includes paying attention to the needs of the world. In *Beyond the University: Why Liberal Education Matters*, Michael Roth writes, "Critical thinking is **sterile**[23] without the capacity for **empathy**[24] and comprehension that stretches the self." Humans are made to connect with the moods, feelings, and thoughts of others. The creative skills developed through the liberal arts enhance our ability to communicate and act on our empathy for the world. An important learning outcome is to sensitize students to the **plight**[25] of the marginalized, the neglected, and the oppressed. Thoughtful leaders recognize abuses of power in order to find creative ways to confront them.

7. Another aspect of leadership is commitment. A true leader who has his or her priorities straight is more committed to the power of principle than to power over others. Through sustained reading and thinking, a liberal arts student has many opportunities to engage with principles. A liberal arts education challenges students to learn to live with themselves, accepting who they are and may become. It lays a foundation for students who seek to live principled lives rather than being persuaded by power or the herd in order to

achieve recognition or **ephemeral**[26] happiness. A potential danger of **aspiring**[27] to leadership is the temptation to put aside principle—to spin the narrative to maintain constituent **allegiances**[28], to compromise integrity, to cut corners in order to get to the top, to cover things up. Self-reliant individuals will choose the right course even if it means moving down the corporate ladder or falling completely off. True leaders like Elizabeth Cady-Stanton, Frederick Douglass, W. E. B. Du Bois, Martin Luther King Jr., and 1960s activist Mario Savio demonstrate by example to young people how to face incredible opposition in the pursuit of principled living. These leaders had a type of character that made them different from and unwelcome by leaders who sought to sustain the **status quo**[29].

8. These historically self-reliant individuals believed that principle was more important than social respectability, professionalism, education, even their own lives. Yet their commitments did not make them stubborn **dogmatists**[30]. Principled persons demonstrate an awareness of reality and may be convinced to change their minds. They may be **blatantly**[31] wrong, yet they are capable of developing a better way of seeing the world. They are always ready to alter a perspective for the sake of growing in wisdom, in the kind of knowledge that is truly life-affirming. They are not interested in **dissimulating**[32] to give the appearance of consistency, for to do so, as Ralph Waldo Emerson reminds us, would reflect a small and troubled mind. To be "great", Emerson says, "is to be misunderstood." Try incorporating that into a marketing campaign.

(From Ryan McIlhenny's *Reforming the Liberal Art*)

Vocabulary

1. extoll /ɪksˈtɒl/

v. praise 赞美

e.g. She was extolled as a genius.

2. innovative /ˈɪnəveɪtɪv/

adj. new and original 革新的；新颖的

e.g. He was one of the most creative and innovative engineers of his generation.

3. **laudatory** /ˈlɔːdətəri/

adj. expressing praise or admiration for someone（文章或言谈）表示赞美的；颂扬性的

e. g. The newspaper has this very laudatory article about your retirement.

4. **overlook** /ˌəʊvəˈlʊk/

v. not notice, or realize how important it is 忽略；忽视；未注意到

e. g. We overlook all sorts of warning signals about our own health.

5. **proponent** /prəˈpəʊnənt/

n. a supporter of a particular idea or course of action 支持者；拥护者；辩护者

e. g. Halsey was identified as a leading proponent of the values of progressive education.

6. **trope** /trəʊp/

n. a word or phrase that is used in a way that is different from its usual meaning in order to create a particular mental image or effect 修辞；转义词语

7. **manipulative** /məˈnɪpjələtɪv/

adj. skillfully forcing or persuading people to act in the way that they want 操纵的；控制的；善于摆布（他人）的

e. g. He described Mr Long as cold, calculating and manipulative.

8. **churn out**

produce large quantities very quickly 快速生产；大量生产

e. g. He began to churn out literary compositions in English.

9. **plethora** /ˈpleθərə/

n. a large amount, especially an amount that is greater than is needed or wanted 大量；（尤指）过多；过剩

e. g. A plethora of new machines will be allowed to enter the market and we will have more choices.

10. **contradiction** /ˌkɒntrəˈdɪkʃn/

n. a confusing or difficult situation where one aspect is completely different from other aspects 矛盾；不一致

e. g. His public speeches are in direct contradiction to his personal lifestyle, so people begin to have doubts about what he has said. They can't trust him any more.

11. **deficit** /ˈdefɪsɪt/

n. the amount by which something is less than what is required or expected, especially the amount by which the total money received is less than the total money spent 差额；赤字；亏损

12. **matriculation** /məˌtrɪkjuˈleɪʃn/

n. the act of registering formally as a student at a university, or the state of satisfying the academic requirements necessary for registration for a course 注册入学；被录取入学

13. **rally** /ˈræli/

v. unite to support 一致支持；集合起来；召集

e. g. His supporters have rallied to his defense.

14. **initiate** /ɪˈnɪʃieɪt, ɪˈnɪʃiət/

v. start or cause to happen 开始；创始；发起

e. g. They wanted to initiate a discussion on economics.

15. **heed** /hiːd/

v. pay attention to and do what is suggested 注意；留心；听从

e. g. She didn't heed my advice and ran into big trouble.

16. **insight** /ˈɪnsaɪt/

n. the ability to understand complex situations 洞察力

e. g. He was a man with considerable insight.

17. **telos** /ˈtelɒs/

n. aim；end 终极；目的

18. **dictatorial** /ˌdɪktəˈtɔːriəl/

adj. controlled or used by a dictator 独裁的；专政的

19. **expend** /ɪkˈspend/

v. use or spend 花费；耗费

e. g. Children expend a lot of energy and may need more high-energy food than adults.

20. **antebellum** /ˌæntɪˈbeləm/

adj. before the American Civil War 美国内战前的

21. **transform** /trænsˈfɔːm/

v. make someone or something completely different, usually in a way that makes them more attractive, easier to use, etc 使改变形态

e. g. It was an event that would transform my life.

22. **woefully** /ˈwəʊfəli/

adv. sadly 悲惨地；忧伤地

e. g. He did this woefully because he had lost his beloved.

23. **sterile** /ˈsteraɪl/

adj. lacking in energy and new ideas 无生气的；缺乏新意的

e. g. Too much time has been wasted in sterile debate.

24. **empathy** /ˈempəθi/

n. the ability to share another person's feelings and emotions 共情；同情

e. g. Having begun my life in a children's home, I have great empathy with the little ones.

25. **plight** /plaɪt/

n. difficult or distressing situation that is full of problems 困境；苦境

e. g. He was in a sorry plight when he became ill and had no money.

26. ephemeral /ɪˈfemərəl/

adj. lasting only for a very short time 短暂的;瞬间的;转瞬即逝的

e. g. These paintings are in some ways a reminder that earthly pleasures are ephemeral.

27. aspire /əˈspaɪə(r)/

v. have a strong desire to achieve something 向往;渴望;有志于

e. g. They aspired to be gentlemen, though they were far from reaching the standard that most people agreed on.

28. allegiance /əˈliːdʒəns/

n. support for and loyalty to a particular group, person, or belief 忠诚;拥护

e. g. My allegiance to Kendall and his company ran deep.

29. status quo /ˌsteɪtəs ˈkwəʊ/

the state of affairs that exists at a particular time 现状;原状

e. g. They have no wish for any change in the status quo.

30. dogmatist /ˈdɒgmətɪst/

n. people who state things strongly without considering all the relevant facts or other people's opinions 教条主义者

e. g. We cannot allow dogmatists to stand in the way of progress.

31. blatantly /ˈbleɪtəntli/

adv. to add emphasis when you are describing states or situations which you think are bad (强调糟糕) 非常;极为;完全

e. g. For years, blatantly false assertions have gone unchallenged.

32. dissimulate /dɪˈsɪmjuleɪt/

v. hide true feelings, intentions, or nature 掩盖;掩饰(情感或动机)

e. g. He didn't attempt to dissimulate or conceal his true feelings.

Exercises for Text 2

I. Decide whether the statements are true (T) or false (F) according to the text.

1. People with critical thinking will not be liked by those in power in the USA.
2. A leader can organize people for doing what is right.
3. Liberal arts offer the freedom to promote the development of self and world.
4. Since true leaders stick to principle, they will never compromise their principle in any circumstance.
5. A liberal arts education helps students to learn to accept themselves.

II. Translate the following sentences with the key words in the parentheses.

1. 非洲象正面临绝境,我们应该采取措施保护它们。(plight)
2. 由于我们对他提供了帮助,因此他决定向我们表示忠诚。(allegiance)
3. 他很容易就获得了名望,但名望因此也转瞬即逝。(ephemeral)
4. 上周在伦敦召开的大会上,几乎没有人留意他的警告。(heed)
5. 这次旅行由社区活动中心的经理发起。(initiate)
6. 贝丝谈及哈默医生时赞不绝口。(laudatory)
7. 我突然明白了这个梦意味着什么。(insight)
8. 这种论点即使不完全是谬误,但也是误导人的。(fallacious)
9. 护士应当努力与病人建立心理上的沟通。(empathy)
10. 我们的新老板主张,员工会议应当简短,但要经常开。(proponent)

III. Explain the following sentences in your own words.

1. These well-trained individuals think outside the textbook, so to speak, and beyond the narrow confines of a specific major.
2. Packing the market with leaders would create a leadership deficit.
3. The sad reality is that many, particularly those under the influence of corporate power, rarely support leaders who seek the betterment of the world.
4. Too many educators simply hand students good grades or are pressured to do so by students themselves or dictatorial administrators.
5. To be "great", Emerson says, "is to be misunderstood."

Learning Strategies

Predicting the Content from the Title

To predict is to guess what comes next. It helps us understand what kinds of articles we are reading. When we read an article, we can often predict the content from the title.

For example, the title of Text 1 is "Who Killed the Liberal Arts?".

From this title, we can predict:

1. This article is about liberal arts.
2. Since it uses a question, the writer might not be satisfied with the education of liberal arts.

Therefore, the article is most probably about the problem in the education of liberal arts.

Now you can use this learning strategy to predict what the second text is about according to the information contained in the title.

Unit Project

With some technology companies of China suppressed by the USA, lots of articles talk about the importance of science. Some articles even claim that students studying liberal arts are not as useful as those studying science. Lots of universities are deciding to cut liberal arts courses. Work in groups to discuss articles talking about liberal arts and write a letter to the university principal, telling him your ideas about the importance of liberal arts courses in the university.

1. Find articles talking about liberal arts and sum up their views.
2. Hold a discussion in groups about whether you agree with the views of those articles.
3. Give an analysis of those articles by using the two authors' view in Text 1 and Text 2.
4. Sum up the view of group members and write a letter to the principal about the importance of liberal arts courses in the university.

Unit 3

Ancient Educational Wisdom

Pre-reading questions:

1. What do you know about Plato and Confucius's views on education?
2. What educational ideas of these two philosophers impress you the most?

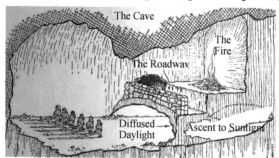

>>> Unit 3 Ancient Educational Wisdom

Text 1

Republic

Plato

1. Now then, I **proceeded**[1] to say, go on to compare our natural condition, so far as education and ignorance are concerned, to a state of things like the following. Imagine a number of men living in an underground cavernous chamber, with an entrance open to the light extending along the entire length of the **cavern**[2], in which they have been **confined**[3], from their childhood, with their legs and necks so **shackled**[4] that they are **obliged**[5] to sit still and look straight forwards, because their chains **render**[6] it impossible for them to turn their heads round; and imagine a bright fire burning some way off, above and behind them, and an **elevated**[7] roadway passing between the fire and the prisoners, with a low wall built along it, like the screens which **conjurors**[8] put up in front of their audience, and above which they exhibit their wonders.

2. I have it, he replied.

3. Also figure to yourself a number of persons walking behind this wall, and carrying with them statues of men and images of other animals, **wrought**[9] in wood and stone and all kinds of materials, together with various other articles, which **overtop**[10] the wall; and as you might expect, let some of the passers-by be talking, and others silent.

4. You are describing a strange scene, and strange prisoners.

5. They resemble us, I replied. For let me ask you, in the first place, whether persons so confined could have seen anything of themselves or of each other beyond the shadows thrown by the fire upon the part of cavern facing them?

6. Certainly not, if you suppose them to have been compelled all their lifetime to keep their heads unmoved.

7. And is not their knowledge of the things carried past them equally limited?

8. Unquestionably it is.

9. And if they were able to **converse**[11] with one another, do you not think that they would be in the habit of giving names to the objects which they saw before them?

10. Doubtless they would.

11. Again: if their prison-house returned an **echo**[12] from the part facing them whenever one of the passers-by opened his lips, to what, let me ask you, could they refer the voice, if not to the shadow which was passing?

12. Unquestionably they would refer it to that.

13. Then surely such persons would hold the shadows of those manufactured articles to be the only realities.

14. Without a doubt they would.

15. Now consider what would happen if the course of nature brought them a **release**[13] from their **fetters**[14], and a **remedy**[15] for their foolishness, in the following manner. Let us suppose that one of them has been released, and compelled suddenly to stand up, and turn his neck round and walk with open eyes towards the light; and let us suppose that he goes through all these actions with pain, and that the **dazzling**[16] splendour renders him incapable of discerning those objects of which he used **formerly**[17] to see the shadows. What answer should you expect him to make if someone were to tell him that in those days he was watching foolish **phantoms**[18], but that now he is somewhat nearer to reality, and is turned towards things more real, and sees more correctly; above all, if he were to point out to him the several objects that are passing by, and question him, and compel him to answer what they are, should you not expect him to be puzzled, and to regard his old visions as truer than the objects now forced upon his notice?

16. Yes, much truer.

17. And if he were further compelled to gaze at the light itself, would not his eyes, think you, be **distressed**[19], and would he not **shrink**[20] and turn away to the things which he could see **distinctly**[21], and consider them to be really clearer than the things pointed out to him?

18. Just so.

19. And if someone were to drag him violently up the rough and **steep**[22] **ascent**[23] from the cavern, and refuse to let him go till he had drawn him out

>>> Unit 3　Ancient Educational Wisdom

into the light of the sun, would he not, think you, be **vexed**[24] and **indignant**[25] at such treatment, and on reaching the light, would he not find his eyes so **dazzled**[26] by the glare as to be incapable of making out so much as one of the objects that are now called true?

20. Yes, he would find it so at first.

21. Hence, I suppose, habit will be necessary to enable him to **perceive**[27] objects in that upper world. At first, he will be most successful in **distinguishing**[28] shadows; then he will discern the **reflections**[29] of men and other things in water, and afterwards the realities; and after this he will raise his eyes to encounter the light of the moon and stars, finding it less difficult to study the **heavenly**[30] bodies and the heaven itself by night than the sun and the sun's light by day.

22. Doubtless.

23. Last of all, I imagine, he will be able to observe and **contemplate**[31] the nature of the sun, not as it appears in water or on **alien**[32] ground, but as it is in itself in its own **territory**[33].

24. Of course.

25. His next step will be to draw the conclusion that the sun is the **author**[34] of the seasons and the years, and the **guardian**[35] of all things in the **visible**[36] world, and in a manner the cause of all those things that he and his companions used to see.

26. Obviously, this will be his next step.

27. What then? When he recalls to mind his first **habitation**[37], and the wisdom of the place, and his old fellow-prisoners, do you not think he will congratulate himself on the change, and pity them?

28. Assuredly he will.

29. And if it was their practice in those days to receive honour and **commendations**[38] one from another, and to give prizes to him who had the keenest eye for a passing object, and who remembered best all that used to **precede**[39] and follow and accompany it, and from those data **divined**[40] most ably what was going to come next, do you fancy that he will **covet**[41] these prizes, and envy those who receive honour and exercise authority among them? Do you not rather imagine that he will feel what Homer describes, and wish extremely "To **drudge**[42] on the lands of a master, under a **portionless**[43] **wight**[44]", and be ready to go through anything rather than entertain those opinions and live in that fashion?

30. For my own part, he replied, I am quite of that opinion. I believe he would consent to go through anything rather than live in that way.

31. And now consider what would happen if such a man were to **descend**[45] again and seat himself on his old seat. Coming so suddenly out of the sun, would he not find his eyes blinded with the gloom of the place?

32. Certainly he would.

33. And if he were forced to **deliver**[46] his opinion again, touching the shadows **aforesaid**[47], and to enter the lists against those who had always been prisoners, while his sight continued **dim**[48] and his eyes unsteady—and if this process of **initiation**[49] lasted a **considerable**[50] time—would he not be made a laughing-stock, and would it not be said of him that he had gone up only to come back again with his eyesight destroyed, and that it was not **worthwhile**[51] even to attempt the ascent? And if anyone **endeavored**[52] to set them free and carry them to the light, would they not go so far as to put him to death, if they could only manage to get him into their power?

34. Yes, that they would.

35. Now this imaginary case, my dear Glaucon, you must apply in all its parts to our former statements, by comparing the region which the eye reveals to the prison-house, and the light of the fire therein to the power of the sun: and if by the upward ascent and the contemplation of the upper world you understand the mounting of the soul into the intellectual region, you will hit the tendency of my own **surmises**[53], since you desire to be told what they are, though indeed, God only knows whether they are correct. But be that as it may, the view which I take of the subject is to the following effect. In the world of knowledge, the essential Form of Good is the limit of our inquiries, and can barely be perceived, but when perceived, we cannot help concluding that it is in every case the source of all that is bright and beautiful—in the visible world giving birth to light and its master, and in the intellectual world **dispensing**[54], immediately and with full authority, truth and reason; and that whosoever would act wisely, either in private or in public, must set this Form of Good before his eyes.

36. To the best of my power, said he, I quite agree with you.

37. That being the case, I continued, pray agree with me on another point, and do not be surprised that those who have climbed so high are

>>> Unit 3 Ancient Educational Wisdom

unwilling to take a part in the affairs of men, because their souls are ever **loath**[55] to desert that upper region. For how could it be otherwise, if the preceding simile is indeed a correct representation of their case?

38. True, it could scarcely be otherwise.

39. Well, do you think it a marvelous thing that a person who has just quitted the contemplation of divine objects for the study of human **infirmities**[56], should betray awkwardness, and appear very ridiculous, when with his sight still dazed and before he has become sufficiently habituated to the darkness that reigns around, he finds himself compelled to contend in courts of law, or elsewhere, about the shadows of justice, or images which throw the shadows, and to enter the lists in questions involving the arbitrary suppositions entertained by those who have never yet had a glimpse of the essential features of justice?

40. No, it is anything but marvelous.

(This is a conversation between Plato and his cousin Glaucon taken from the seventh volume of his *Republic*.)

Vocabulary

1. **proceed** /prəˈsiːd/

v. continue to 接下来做;接着做

e. g. He proceeded to tell me things related to my birth.

2. **cavern** /ˈkævən/

n. a large deep cave 大地穴;大洞穴

3. **confine** /kənˈfaɪn/

v. keep someone or something within limits 限制(自己或自己的活动);使受局限

e. g. He did not confine himself to the language.

4. **shackle** /ˈʃækl/

v. put shackles on; prevent someone from doing what they want to do 给……上镣铐;束缚;阻挠

e. g. She was shackled to a wall.

People find themselves shackled to a high-stress job.

5. **oblige** /əˈblaɪdʒ/

v. make it necessary for someone to do something 强迫;迫使

45

e. g. The storm got worse and worse. Finally, I was obliged to abandon the car and continue on foot.

6. render /ˈrendə(r)/

v. change something into certain state 致使；造成

e. g. It contained so many errors as to render it worthless.

7. elevate /ˈelɪveɪt/

v. raise something above a horizontal level 举起；抬起；使升高

e. g. We should elevate the quality in order to enlarge the sales amount.

8. conjuror /ˈkʌndʒərə(r)/

n. someone who performs magic tricks to amuse an audience 魔术师；行咒法者

9. wrought /rɔːt/

adj. created in that material or way 以……原料制造的；以……方式制作的

10. overtop /ˌəʊvəˈtɒp/

v. rise above the top of; be superior to 高于；胜过

11. converse /kənˈvɜːs/

v. talk 交谈；说话

e. g. Luke sat directly behind the pilot and conversed with him.

12. echo /ˈekəʊ/

n. a noise that is repeated because the sound hits a surface and returns 回响

13. release /rɪˈliːs/

v. set something free or allow it to go 释放；放出

e. g. He was released from custody the next day.

14. fetter /ˈfetə/

n. chains for a prisoner's feet 脚镣

15. remedy /ˈremədi/

n. a successful way of dealing with a problem（问题的）解决方法；解决良方

e. g. The remedy lies in the hands of the company.

16. dazzling /ˈdæzlɪŋ/

adj. so bright that it makes people unable to see for a short period of time 耀眼的；晃眼睛的

17. formerly /ˈfɔːməli/

adv. happening or being true in the past 从前；原来；以前

e. g. He had formerly been in the Navy.

18. phantom /ˈfæntəm/

n. something which someone thinks they experience but which is not real 幻觉；幻象

19. distressed /dɪˈstrest/

adj. upset or worried 烦恼的；忧虑的

Unit 3 Ancient Educational Wisdom

e. g. At the end of it all, Alex is no longer able to listen to his favorite music without feeling distressed.

20. shrink /ʃrɪŋk/

v. move away because frightened, shocked, or disgusted（因害怕、震惊或厌恶）退缩；畏缩；避开

e. g. One child shrank away from me when I tried to talk to him.

21. distinctly /dɪsˈtɪŋktli/

adv. clearly 清楚地；清晰地；明显地

e. g. He was beginning to feel distinctly uneasy about their visit.

22. steep /stiːp/

adj. rising at a very sharp angle and difficult to go up 陡的；陡峭的；陡直的

e. g. San Francisco is built on 40 hills and some are very steep.

23. ascent /əˈsent/

n. an upward slope or path, especially when walking or climbing 上坡路；上坡

24. vex /veks/

v. make someone feel annoyed, puzzled, and frustrated 使恼火；使困惑；使伤脑筋

e. g. Everything about her vexed him.

25. indignant /ɪnˈdɪɡnənt/

adj. shocked and angry, because something is unjust or unfair 愤怒的；愤慨的

e. g. She wrote an indignant letter to the editor.

26. dazzle /ˈdæzl/

v. make someone unable to see properly for a short time（强光等）使目眩；使眼花

27. perceive /pəˈsiːv/

v. see, notice, or realize something, especially when it is not obvious 注意到；察觉；意识到（尤指不明显之物）

28. distinguish /dɪˈstɪŋɡwɪʃ/

v. recognize the difference between two people or things 觉察出；知道；了解

29. reflection /rɪˈflekʃn/

n. an image that you see when you look in a mirror or other shiny surface; deep thinking 映象；沉思

e. g. She was looking at her reflection in the mirror.

On/Upon reflection, I decided to accept their offer.

30. heavenly /ˈhevnli/

adj. connected with the religious idea of heaven 天堂的；天国的

31. contemplate /ˈkɒntəmpleɪt/

v. think about whether to do something or not; think about carefully for a long time 考虑，思量，思忖；深思熟虑，沉思，苦思冥想

e. g. For a time, he contemplated a career as an army medical doctor.

47

As he lay in his hospital bed that night, he cried as he contemplated his future.

32. **alien** /ˈeɪliən/

adj. not familiar or like other things you have known; different from what you are used to 陌生的;格格不入的

e. g. She felt lost in an alien culture when she moved to the city.

33. **territory** /ˈterətri/

n. land which is controlled by a particular country or ruler 领土;领地

34. **author** /ˈɔːθə/

n. the person who creates or starts something, especially a plan or an idea 发起人;发起物

e. g. She is the author of a plan for reforming the school system.

35. **guardian** /ˈɡɑːdiən/

n. someone who defends and protects 保护者;护卫者

36. **visible** /ˈvɪzəbl/

adj. that can be seen 可见的;看得见的

e. g. The ship was not visible through the fog.

37. **habitation** /ˌhæbɪˈteɪʃn/

n. a place where people live 住处;住所;聚居地

38. **commendation** /ˌkɒmenˈdeɪʃn/

n. the act of praising or approving of someone or something; something (such as an official letter) that praises someone publicly 赞扬;奖状

e. g. Their hard work deserves commendation.

The President issued a commendation praising the volunteers for their exceptional work during the relief effort.

39. **precede** /prɪˈsiːd/

v. happen before 发生在……之前;先于

e. g. The earthquake was preceded by a loud roar and lasted 20 seconds.

40. **divine** /dɪˈvaɪn/

v. predict 预言;推论;推测

41. **covet** /ˈkʌvət/

v. strongly want to have something for oneself 渴望;贪求;觊觎

e. g. She coveted his job so openly that conversations between them were tense. Their relationship became worse.

42. **drudge** /drʌdʒ/

v. work hard at a job which is not very important or interesting 做苦力

43. **portionless** /ˈpɔːʃnlɪs/

adj. having no dowry or inheritance 没有嫁妆的;没有继承财产的

44. wight /waɪt/

n. (archaic term) a human being 〈古〉人；人类

45. descend /dɪˈsend/

v. move downwards from a higher level to a lower level 下来；下降；走下

e.g. She descended one flight of stairs.

46. deliver /dɪˈlɪvə/

v. do, make, or produce 履行；兑现

e.g. He will deliver the speech at noon.

47. aforesaid /əˈfɔːsed/

adj. aforementioned 之前提到的

e.g. Based on the aforesaid reasons, the court has come to its decision.

48. dim /dɪm/

adj. not bright 昏暗的；暗淡的

e.g. I found her sitting in a dim corner of the restaurant.

49. initiation /ɪˌnɪʃɪˈeɪʃn/

n. the starting of something 开始；创始

e.g. They announced the initiation of a rural development programme.

50. considerable /kənˈsɪdərəbl/

adj. great in amount or degree 相当多的；相当大的

e.g. Though in some cases it has taken considerable genius to realize their first application, they're easy to understand.

51. worthwhile /ˌwɜːθˈwaɪl/

adj. enjoyable or useful, and being worth the time, money, or effort that is spent on it 有价值的；令人愉快的；值得花费时间（或金钱、精力）的

e.g. The money is for a worthwhile cause.

52. endeavor /ɪnˈdevə/

v. try very hard to do 努力；尽力

e.g. The school endeavors to teach students to be good citizens.

53. surmise /səˈmaɪz, ˈsɜːmaɪz/

v. form an opinion about something without definitely knowing the truth 推测；猜测

e.g. He surmised that he had discovered one of the illegal streets.

54. dispense /dɪˈspens/

v. give or provide 分配；分发；施与

e.g. A newspaper columnist dispenses advice to millions of readers each week.

55. loath /ləʊθ/

adj. not wanting or willing to do something 不乐意；不情愿的；勉强的

e.g. She is loath to give up her hard-earned liberty.

56. infirmity /ɪnˈfɜːməti/

n. the quality or state of being weak or ill especially because of old age; a disease or illness that usually lasts for a long time 弱点;缺点;虚弱;疾病

e. g. We all fear disability or infirmity.

Exercises for Text 1

I. Read the text and answer the questions.

1. What is the prisoner asked to do in the beginning? How does he feel at first?
2. How does he feel when he stays outside for some time?
3. What happens when he comes back to the cave? How does he feel about it?
4. What do other prisoners think of him?
5. What are the implications of this story to our education?

II. Complete the sentences with the words below. Change the form where necessary.

considerable	perceive	endeavour	indignant	worthwhile
initiation	converse	precede	oblige	descend
release	proceed	vex	confine	reflection
surmise	shackle	make demands on	render	contemplate

1. Doing it properly _____ our time, but unfortunately, we do not have so much time.
2. The project wasted a(n) _____ amount of time and money.
3. They are _____ to change the plan totally, but they will not succeed.
4. It was a(n) _____ movie that was interesting enough to make us watch it again.
5. There was a year between _____ and completion.
6. The plan crash was _____ by the scary scream of desperate people.
7. Things are cooler and more damp as we _____ to the cellar.
8. He is expected to be _____ from hospital today.
9. It _____ me to think of others gossiping behind my back.
10. We _____ that the delay was caused by some accident and later our guess was proved.
11. She _____ leaving for the sake of the kids. Many people try to persuade her out of this.
12. I couldn't _____ any difference between these coins no matter how hard I tried.
13. He is _____ at the suggestions that he has done nothing right.

14. They were _____ in German, their only common language.
15. Her job _____ her to work overtime and on weekends.
16. He outlined his plans and then _____ to explain them in more detail.
17. Yoko had largely _____ her activities to the world of big business. It was efficient, but it also made her lose the chance in the world of small business.
18. Many young people are _____ to their jobs and have no time to date.
19. The car accident _____ his brother disabled and put his family in pain.
20. These two works demonstrate Gilman's _____ and exploration of female autonomy from different perspectives.

III. Translate the sentences into Chinese.

1. For let me ask you, in the first place, whether persons so confined could have seen anything of themselves or of each other beyond the shadows thrown by the fire upon the part of cavern facing them?
2. And if they were able to converse with one another, do you not think that they would be in the habit of giving names to the objects which they saw before them?
3. If their prison-house returned an echo from the part facing them whenever one of the passers-by opened his lips, to what, let me ask you, could they refer the voice, if not to the shadow which was passing?
4. Now consider what would happen if the course of nature brought them a release from their fetters, and a remedy for their foolishness, in the following manner.
5. Should you not expect him to be puzzled, and to regard his old visions as truer than the objects now forced upon his notice?

Text 2

The Analects

Confucius

1. The Master said, "Having studied, to then repeatedly apply what you have learned—is this not a source of pleasure? To have friends come from distant quarters—is this not a source of enjoyment? To go unacknowledged by others without **harboring**[1] frustration—is this not the mark of an exemplary person (junzi)?"

2. Master You said, "It is a rare thing for someone who has a sense of **filial**[2] and **fraternal**[3] responsibility (xiaoti) to have a taste for **defying**[4] authority. And it is unheard of for those who have no taste for defying authority to be keen on **initiating**[5] rebellion. Exemplary persons (junzi) concentrate their efforts on the root, for the root having taken hold, the way (dao) will grow therefrom. As for filial and fraternal responsibility, it is, I suspect, the root of authoritative conduct (ren)."

3. The Master said, "It is a rare thing for glib speech and an **insinuating**[6] appearance to accompany **authoritative**[7] conduct (ren)."

4. Master Zeng said, "Daily I examine my person on three counts. In my undertakings on behalf of other people, have I failed to do my utmost (zhong)? In my interactions with colleagues and friends, have I failed to make good on my word (xin)? In what has been passed on to me, have I failed to carry it into practice?"

5. The Master said, "As a younger brother and son, be filial (xiao) at home and deferential (ti) in the community; be cautious in what you say and then make good on your word (xin); love the multitude broadly and be intimate with those who are authoritative in their conduct (ren). If in so behaving you still have energy left, use it to improve yourself through study."

6. Zixia said, "As for persons who care for character much more than beauty, who in serving their parents are able to **exert**[8] themselves utterly,

who give their whole person in the service of their ruler, and who, in interactions with colleagues and friends, **make good on**[9] their word (xin)—even if it were said of such persons that they are unschooled, I would insist that they are well-educated indeed."

7. The Master said, "Exemplary persons (junzi) lacking in gravity would have no dignity. Yet in their studies they are not inflexible. Take doing your utmost and making good on your word (xin) as your mainstay. Do not have as a friend anyone who is not as good as you are. And where you have erred, do not hesitate to mend your ways."...

8. The Master said, "From fifteen, my heart-and-mind was set upon learning; from thirty I took my stance; from forty I was no longer doubtful; from fifty I realized the **propensities**[10] of tian (tianming); from sixty my ear was **attuned**[11]; from seventy I could give my heart-and-mind free rein without overstepping the boundaries."...

9. The Master said, "Reviewing the old as a means of realizing the new—such a person can be considered a teacher."...

10. The Master said, "Exemplary persons (junzi) are not mere vessels."...

11. Zigong asked about exemplary persons (junzi). The Master replied, "They first accomplish what they are going to say, and only then say it."...

12. The Master said, "Learning without due reflection leads to **perplexity**[12]; reflection without learning leads to **perilous**[13] circumstances."

13. The Master said, "To become **accomplished**[14] in some **heterodox**[15] doctrine will bring nothing but harm."

14. The Master said, "Zilu, shall I teach you what wisdom (zhi) means?" To know (zhi) what you know and know what you do not know—this then is wisdom."

15. Zizhang was studying in order to take office. The Master said, "If you listen broadly, set aside what you are unsure of, and speak **cautiously**[16] on the rest, you will make few errors; if you look broadly, set aside what is perilous, and act cautiously on the rest, you will have few regrets. To speak with few errors and to act with few regrets is the substance of taking office."...

16. The Master said, "The exemplary person (junzi) wants to be slow to speak yet quick to act."...

17. Zaiwo was still sleeping during the daytime. The Master said, "You cannot carve rotten wood, and cannot **trowel**[17] over a wall of **manure**[18]. As for Zaiwo, what is the point in **upbraiding**[19] him?" The Master said further, "There was a time when, in my dealings with others, on hearing what they had to say, I believed they would live up to it. Nowadays in my dealings with others, on hearing what they have to say, I then watch what they do. It is Zaiwo that has taught me as much." …

18. The Master said, "I do not open the way for students who are not driven with eagerness; I do not supply a vocabulary for students who are not trying desperately to find the language for their ideas. If on showing students one corner they do not come back to me with the other three, I will not repeat myself." …

19. The Master said, "In strolling in the company of just two other persons, I am bound to find a teacher. Identifying their strengths, I follow them, and identifying their weaknesses, I reform myself accordingly." …

20. The Master said, "How would I dare to consider myself a sage (sheng) or an authoritative person (ren)? What can be said about me is simply that I continue my studies without **respite**[20] and instruct others without growing weary." Gongxi Hua remarked, "It is precisely this **commitment**[21] that we students are unable to learn." …

21. The Master said, "The exemplary person (junzi) is calm and **unperturbed**[22]; the **petty**[23] person is always **agitated**[24] and anxious." …

22. The Master said, "Study as though you cannot catch up to it, and as though you fear you are going to lose it." …

23. The Master said, "The exemplary person (junzi) helps to bring out the best in others, but does not help to bring out the worst. The petty person does just the opposite." …

24. Zigong inquired about how to treat friends, and the Master replied, "Do your **utmost**[25] (zhong) to **exhort**[26] them, and lead them **adeptly**[27] (shan) along the way (dao). But if they are unwilling, then desist—don't disgrace yourself in the process." …

25. The Master said, "The person who does not consider what is still far off will not escape being alarmed at what is near at hand."

(From *The Analects of Confucius*, a philosophical translation translated by Roger T. Ames and Henry Rosemont)

>>> Unit 3 Ancient Educational Wisdom

Vocabulary

1. harbor /ˈhɑːbə/

v. have something in someone's mind over a long period of time 心怀；怀藏；怀有

e. g. Tom harbors no regrets after doing it.

2. filial /ˈfɪliəl/

adj. dutiful to parents 孝顺的

e. g. His father accused him of neglecting his filial duties because he hardly cared about his parents.

3. fraternal /frəˈtɜːnl/

adj. showing strong links of friendship between two people or groups of people 兄弟的；兄弟般的；友爱的

e. g. The fraternal assistance of our colleagues are very helpful.

4. defy /dɪˈfaɪ/

v. refuse to obey 违抗；反抗；不服从

e. g. She defied her parents and dropped out of school.

5. initiate /ɪˈnɪʃieɪt, ɪˈnɪʃiət/

v. start something or cause it to happen 开始；创始；发起

e. g. They wanted to initiate a discussion on economics.

6. insinuating /ɪnˈsɪnjueɪtɪŋ/

adj. winning favor and confidence by imperceptible degrees 曲意巴结的

7. authoritative /ɔːˈθɒrətətɪv/

adj. of recognized authority or excellence 权威的；有威信的

8. exert /ɪɡˈzɜːt/

v. make a great physical or mental effort, or work hard to do something 尽力；努力

e. g. Do not exert yourself unnecessarily.

9. make good on

realize; live up to 实现；兑现

e. g. I'll make good on my promise.

10. propensity /prəˈpensəti/

n. a natural tendency that you have to behave in a particular way（性格上的）倾向；习性

e. g. She hasn't reckoned on his propensity for violence.

11. attuned /əˈtjuːnd/

adj. being able to understand and appreciate 适应的；理解的

e. g. He seemed unusually attuned to people's feelings.

12. perplexity /pəˈpleksəti/

n. a feeling of being confused and frustrated because someone does not understand something 困惑；迷惘

e. g. He began counting on them and then, with growing perplexity, counted on them a second time.

13. perilous /ˈperələs/

adj. very dangerous 危险的；艰险的

e. g. The road grew even steeper and more perilous.

14. accomplished /əˈkʌmplɪʃt/

adj. very good at a particular thing; having a lot of skills 才华高的；有造诣的

e. g. She is an accomplished painter.

15. heterodox /ˈhetərədɒks/

adj. different from the accepted or official ones 异端的；离经叛道的

16. cautiously /ˈkɔːʃəsli/

adv. acting very carefully in order to avoid possible danger 谨慎地；慎重地

17. trowel /ˈtraʊəl/

v. use a trowel on 用铲子铲

18. manure /məˈnjʊə(r)/

n. animal faeces, sometimes mixed with chemicals, that is spread on the ground in order to make plants grow healthy and strong 粪肥；肥料

19. upbraid /ʌpˈbreɪd/

v. tell someone that they have done something wrong and criticize them for doing it 责难；非难；责骂

e. g. His mother summoned him, upbraided him, wept and prayed.

20. respite /ˈrespaɪt/

n. a short period of rest from something unpleasant or a short delay before a very unpleasant or difficult situation which may or may not take place（不快事情中的）喘息；缓解；暂息；（不快或困难的）暂缓；暂延

e. g. It was some weeks now since they had had any respite from shellfire.

21. commitment /kəˈmɪtmənt/

n. the willingness to work hard and give your energy and time to a job or an activity（对工作或某活动）献身；奉献；投入

e. g. A career as an actor requires one hundred per cent commitment.

22. unperturbed /ˌʌnpəˈtɜːbd/

adj. free from emotional agitation or nervous tension 坦然自若的

e. g. She was unperturbed by the sudden change in plan.

23. petty /ˈpeti/

adj. caring too much about small, unimportant things 小气的；狭隘的；过于关注琐事的

e. g. He was petty-minded and obsessed with detail.

24. agitated /ˈædʒɪteɪtɪd/

adj. very worried or upset 焦虑的；烦恼的；不安的

e.g. Calm down! Don't get so agitated.

25. utmost /ˈʌtməʊst/

n. the state of trying as hard as one can to do it 极度；极限；最大可能

e.g. She was certain that he would have done his utmost to help her.

26. exhort /ɪɡˈzɔːt/

v. try hard to persuade or encourage someone to do something 规劝；劝诫

e.g. Kennedy exhorted his listeners to turn away from violence.

27. adeptly /əˈdeptli, ˈædeptli/

adv. skillfully 内行地；熟练地；擅长地

e.g. He switched adeptly between English and Italian.

Exercises for Text 2

I. Decide whether the statements are true (T) or false (F) according to the text.

1. Confucianism proposes that reviewing can make a person become a teacher.
2. Confucius thinks that we can only teach students when they are eager to learn.
3. According to Confucius, we should immediately help students to express their ideas when they can't express themselves appropriately.
4. Confucius asks us to learn from people around us.
5. In Confucian view, since the most important thing is the present, we don't need to think about the future.

II. Translate the following sentences with the key words in the parentheses.

1. 他劝诫同伴说："要通过勤奋努力实现自己的目标。"（exhort）
2. 他将会用自己的传统医学知识尽全力帮助他们。（utmost）
3. 他批评团队未竭尽全力。（commitment）
4. 他是我们这个时代最杰出的作曲家之一。（accomplished）
5. 宾特先生习惯拖到最后时刻才做决定。（propensity）
6. 他相信盟友们会履行他们的承诺。（make good on）
7. 年轻人如此地沉浸其中，他们没有意识到自己有多么努力。（exert）
8. 这次旅行由社区活动中心的经理发起。（initiate）
9. 这是我第一次勇敢反抗我的母亲。（defy）
10. 他可能被某个对他怀恨在心的人谋杀了。（harbor）

III. Explain the following sentences in your own words.

1. Zigong asked about exemplary persons (junzi). The Master replied, "They first accomplish what they are going to say, and only then say it."

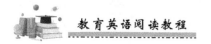

2. Learning without due reflection leads to perplexity; reflection without learning leads to perilous circumstances.
3. The exemplary person (junzi) is calm and unperturbed; the petty person is always agitated and anxious.
4. The exemplary person (junzi) helps to bring out the best in others, but does not help to bring out the worst. The petty person does just the opposite.
5. The exemplary person (junzi) wants to be slow to speak yet quick to act.

Learning Strategies

Guessing the Meaning of a Word from the Context

When we read, sometimes we can guess the meaning of a new word from the context.

If a new word appears in a sentence, when we look at the words before and after the new word, it is possible to find its meaning. For example,

Also figure to yourself a number of persons walking behind this wall, and carrying with them statues of men and images of other animals, **wrought** in wood and stone and all kinds of materials, together with various other articles, which overtop the wall; and as you might expect, let some of the passers-by be talking, and others silent.

In the sentence above, "statue" gives us the hint about the meaning of the word **wrought**.

If the sentence does not help us to get the meaning of a word, we can determine the word's part of speech. Then we can look at the way other words are used in the sentence, as this might give a clue to the meaning of the new word. For example,

And if someone were to drag him violently up the rough and **steep** ascent from the cavern, and refuse to let him go till he had drawn him out into the light of the sun, would he not, think you, be vexed and indignant at such treatment, and on reaching the light, would he not find his eyes so dazzled by the glare as to be incapable of making out so much as one of the objects that are now called true?

In the sentence above, when we take a close look, we find **steep** is the feature of the ascent. Therefore, we can make a guess that it might mean "rising or falling quickly".

Now, please explain how you can figure out the meaning of each of the following words in bold type from the context:

1. The sun is the **author** of the seasons and the years, and the guardian of all

things in the visible world, and in a manner the cause of all those things that he and his companions used to see.

2. "To **drudge** on the lands of a master, under a portionless wight", and be ready to go through anything rather than entertain those opinions and live in that fashion?

3. To go unacknowledged by others without **harboring** frustration—is this not the mark of an exemplary person (junzi)?

Unit Project

Work in groups to make research on the articles introducing the educational ideas of ancient sages in Eastern and Western culture and find out which ideas of theirs are still valid in modern times.

1. Find articles about the educational ideas of ancient sages in Eastern and Western culture and sum up their views.
2. Hold a discussion in groups about which ancient views are still applicable in modern times.
3. Compare their views with those of educators in modern times.
4. Sum up the findings of group members and give a presentation about the influence of those ideas.

Unit 4
Teaching and Learning Principles

Pre-reading questions:

1. What teaching and learning principles do you know?
2. What ideas is Comenius most famous for?

>>> Unit 4　Teaching and Learning Principles

Text 1

The Principles of Facility and Thoroughness in Teaching and Learning

John Amos Comenius

1. Nature observes a suitable time for example: a bird that wishes to **multiply**[1] its species does not **set about**[2] it in winter, when everything is **stiff**[3] with cold, nor in summer, when everything is **parched**[4] and **withered**[5] by the heat; nor yet in autumn, when the **vital**[6] force of all creatures **declines**[7] with the sun's declining rays, and a new winter with hostile **mien**[8] is approaching; but in spring, when the sun brings back life and strength to all. Again, the process consists of several steps. While it is yet cold, the bird **conceives**[9] the eggs and warms them inside its body, where they are protected from the cold; when the air grows warmer, it lays them in its nest, but does not hatch them out until the warm season comes, so that the tender chicks may grow accustomed to light and warmth by degrees.

2. **Imitation**—In the same way the gardener takes care to do nothing out of season, he does not, therefore, plant in the winter (because the sap is then in the roots, preparing to mount and **nourish**[10] the plant later on); nor in summer (when the **sap**[11] is already **dispersed**[12] through the branches); nor in autumn (when the sap is retiring to the roots once more); but in spring, when the moisture is beginning to rise from the roots and the upper part of the plant begins to shoot. Later on, too, it is of great importance to the little tree that the right time be chosen for the various operations that are needful, such as **manuring**[13], **pruning**[14], and cutting. Even the tree itself has its proper time for putting forth shoots and blossoms, for growing, and for coming to maturity. In the same manner the careful builder must choose the right time for cutting timber, burning bricks, laying foundations, building, and **plastering**[15] walls, etc.

3. **Deviation**[16]—In direct opposition to this principle, a twofold error is committed in schools.

(ⅰ) The right time for mental exercise is not chosen.

(ⅱ) The exercises are not properly divided, so that all advance may be made through the several stages needful, with any omission. As long as the boy is still a child he cannot be taught, because the roots of his understanding are still too deep below the surface. As soon as he becomes old, it is too late to teach him, because the intellect and the memory are then failing. In middle age it is difficult, because the forces of the intellect are **dissipated**[17] over a variety of objects and are not easily concentrated. The season of youth, therefore, must be chosen. Then life and mind are fresh and gathering strength; then everything is **vigorous**[18] and strikes root deeply.

4. **Rectification**[19]—We conclude, therefore, that

(ⅰ) The education of men should be **commenced**[20] in the springtime of life, that is to say, in boyhood (for boyhood is the equivalent of spring, youth of summer, manhood of autumn, and old age of winter).

(ⅱ) The morning hours are the most suitable for study (for here again the morning is the equivalent of spring, midday of summer, the evening of autumn, and the night of winter).

(ⅲ) All the subjects that are to be learned should be arranged so as to suit the age of the students, that nothing which is beyond their comprehension be given them to learn.

The Principles of Facility in Teaching and in Learning

1. We have already considered the means by which the educationist may **attain**[21] his goal with certainty, we will now proceed to see how these means can be suited to the minds of the pupils, so that their use may be easy and pleasant.

2. Following in the footsteps of nature we find that the process of education will be easy

(ⅰ) If it begins early, before the mind is **corrupted**[22].

(ⅱ) If the mind be duly prepared to receive it.

(ⅲ) If it proceeds from the general to the particular.

(ⅳ) And from what is easy to what is more difficult.

(ⅴ) If the pupil be not overburdened by too many subjects.

(ⅵ) And if progress be slow in every case.

(ⅶ) If the intellect be forced to nothing to which its natural bent does not **incline**[23] it, in accordance with its age and with the right method.

(ⅷ) If everything should be taught through the **medium**[24] of the senses.

(ⅸ) And if the use of everything taught should be continually kept in view.

(ⅹ) If everything should be taught according to one and the same method.

These, I say, are the principles to be adopted if education is to be easy and pleasant.

The Principles of Thoroughness in Teaching and in Learning

1. It is a common complaint that there are few who leave school with a thorough education, and that most men retain nothing but a **veneer**[25], a mere shadow of true knowledge. This complaint is **corroborated**[26] by facts.

2. The cause of this phenomenon appears on investigation to be twofold: either that the schools occupy themselves with insignificant and unimportant studies, to the neglect of those that are more weighty, or that the pupils forget what they have learned, since most of it merely goes through their heads and does not stick **fast**[27] there. This last fault is so common that there are few who do not lament it. For if everything that we have ever read, heard, and mentally appreciated were always ready to hand in our memories, how learned we should appear! We do, it is true, make practical use of much that we have learned, but the amount that we **recollect**[28] is unsatisfactory, and the fact remains that we are continually trying to pour water into a **sieve**[29].

3. But can no cure be found for this? Certainly there can, if once more we go to the school of nature, and investigate the methods that she adopts to give **endurance**[30] to the beings which she has created.

4. I maintain that a method can be found by means of which each person will be enabled to bring into his mental consciousness not only what he has learned, but more as well; since he will recall with ease all that he has learned from teachers or from books, and, at the same time, will be able to pass sound judgment on the **objective**[31] facts to which his information refers.

5. This will be possible:

(ⅰ) If only those subjects that are of real use be taken in hand.

(ⅱ) If these be taught without **digression**[32] or **interruption**[33].

(ⅲ) If a thorough grounding precede instruction in detail.

(ⅳ) If this grounding be carefully given.

(ⅴ) If all that follows be based on this grounding, and on nothing else.

(vi) If in every subject that consists of several parts, these parts be linked together as much as possible.

(vii) If all that comes later be based on what has gone before.

(viii) If great stress be laid on the points of **resemblance**[34] between **cognate**[35] subjects.

(ix) If all studies be arranged with reference to the intelligence and memory of the pupils, and the nature of language.

(x) If knowledge be fixed in the memory by constant practice.

(From John Amos Comenius's *The Great Didactic*)

Vocabulary

1. multiply /ˈmʌltɪplaɪ/

v. increase greatly in number or amount （使）成倍地增加；（使）大量地增加

e.g. Her husband multiplied his demands on her time.

2. set about

begin 开始

e.g. After the earthquake, the people set about rebuilding their homes.

3. stiff /stɪf/

adj. firm or not bending easily 硬的；不易弯曲的

e.g. The windows were stiff and she couldn't get them open.

4. parch /pɑːtʃ/

v. cause to wither or parch from exposure to heat （使）焦干

5. wither /ˈwɪðə(r)/

v. dry up and die 枯萎；凋谢

e.g. The flowers in Isabel's room had withered.

6. vital /ˈvaɪtl/

adj. necessary or very important; very energetic and full of life 必要的；至关重要的；充满活力的；生气勃勃的

e.g. The port is vital to supply relief to millions of drought victims.

7. decline /dɪˈklaɪn/

v. become less in quantity, importance, or strength 下降；减少；衰退；衰落

e.g. The number of staff has declined from 217,000 to 114,000.

8. mien /miːn/

n. general appearance and manner, especially the expression on the face which shows feeling or thinking 仪表;举止;神态;(尤指)面部表情

e.g. It was impossible to tell from his mien whether he was offended.

9. conceive /kənˈsiːv/

v. think of and work out how something can be done; become pregnant 构思;设想;想出;孕育

e.g. She had conceived the idea of a series of novels.

In some small villages, a woman who is unable to conceive might be discriminated against.

10. nourish /ˈnʌrɪʃ/

v. provide someone with the food that is necessary for life, growth, and good health; allow or encourage something to grow 给……提供营养;滋养;滋长;怀有

e.g. The food she eats nourishes both her and the baby.

This current of thought has been nourished by historical tradition.

11. sap /sæp/

n. the watery liquid in plants and trees(植物的)液;汁

12. disperse /dɪˈspɜːs/

v. spread over a wide area; split up(使)分散;(使)散布;(使)散开

e.g. The oil appeared to be dispersing.

The seeds are dispersed by the wind.

13. manure /məˈnjʊə(r)/

v. spread manure, as for fertilization 施肥

14. prune /pruːn/

v. cut off some of the branches so that the tree will grow better the next year 修剪;修整

15. plaster /ˈplɑːstə/

v. cover something with a layer of plaster 涂灰泥于;在……上抹灰浆

16. deviation /ˌdiːviˈeɪʃn/

n. the act of doing something that is different from what people consider to be normal or acceptable 偏常;反常;离经叛道

e.g. Deviation from the norm is not tolerated.

17. dissipate /ˈdɪsɪpeɪt/

v. become less or become less strong until something disappears or goes away completely; waste something in a foolish way(使)消失;消除;驱散;浪费

e.g. The tension in the room had dissipated.

Her father had dissipated her inheritance.

18. **vigorous** /ˈvɪɡərəs/

adj. strong and healthy and full of energy 精力旺盛的；充满活力的

e. g. Take vigorous exercise for several hours a week.

19. **rectification** /ˌrektɪfɪˈkeɪʃn/

n. the act of changing it to make it correct or satisfactory 纠正；修正；矫正

20. **commence** /kəˈmens/

v. begin 开始

e. g. They commenced a systematic search.

21. **attain** /əˈteɪn/

v. gain or achieve, often after a lot of effort（通常指经过努力）获得；达到

e. g. Most of our students attained five "A" grades in their exams.

22. **corrupted** /kəˈrʌptɪd/

adj. behaving in a way that is morally wrong, especially by doing dishonest or illegal things in return for money or power 腐败的；贪污的；受贿的

e. g. It is sad to see a man so corrupted by the desire for money and power.

23. **incline** /ɪnˈklaɪn, ˈɪnklaɪn/

v. be likely to think or act in that way（使）倾向；（使）趋向

e. g. We have found out the factors which incline us towards particular beliefs.

24. **medium** /ˈmiːdiəm/

n. a way or means of expressing ideas or of communicating with people（表现）方式；（交流）手段

e. g. In Sierra Leone, English is used as the medium of instruction for all primary education.

25. **veneer** /vəˈnɪə(r)/

n. a pleasant appearance, or a polite way of behaving that is not sincere 虚饰；伪装；假象

e. g. He was able to fool the world with his veneer of education.

26. **corroborate** /kəˈrɒbəreɪt/

v. provide evidence or information 证实；确证

e. g. Alice corroborated what Blair had said.

27. **fast** /ˈfæst/

adv. in a way that is not easily moved or changed 牢固地

e. g. She held fast to her belief in justice.

28. **recollect** /ˌrekəˈlekt/

v. remember 想起；记起

e. g. Ramona spoke with warmth when she recollected the doctor who used to be at the county hospital.

>>> Unit 4 Teaching and Learning Principles

29. sieve /sɪv/

n. a tool used for separating solids from liquids or larger pieces of something from smaller pieces 滤勺;筛子

30. endurance /ɪnˈdjʊərəns/

n. the ability to continue with an unpleasant or difficult situation, experience, or activity over a long period of time 耐力;忍耐力

e. g. This event tests both physical and mental endurance.

31. objective /əbˈdʒektɪv/

adj. based on facts 客观的;基于事实的

e. g. I find it difficult to be objective where he's concerned.

32. digression /daɪˈɡreʃn/

n. the state of moving away from the subject talked or written about for a while 偏离主题

e. g. This, however, is a digression, from which we must return to Socrates.

33. interruption /ˌɪntəˈrʌpʃn/

n. the act of saying or doing something that causes others to stop 打断

e. g. I managed to work for two hours without interruption.

34. resemblance /rɪˈzembləns/

n. the state of being similar to each other 相似之处;类似之处

e. g. There was a remarkable resemblance between him and Peter.

35. cognate /ˈkɒɡneɪt/

adj. related to each other 同类的;同源的

e. g. German and Dutch are cognate languages.

Exercises for Text 1

I. **Read the text and answer the questions.**

1. What does the principle of imitation mean?
2. What do the principles of facility mean?
3. Which principles of facility are the most reasonable?
4. What do the principles of thoroughness mean?
5. Which principles do you think are still inspiring for modern education?

II. **Complete the sentences with the words below. Change the form where necessary.**

medium	dissipate	resemblance	corroborate	fast
set about	recollect	vital	endurance	attain
nourish	wither	incline	stiff	veneer
disperse	objective	commence	digression	decline

1. Soapy, having decided to go to the Island, at once _____ accomplishing his desire.
2. Industries unable to modernize have been left to _____.
3. Nick Wileman is a school caretaker so it is _____ that he get on well with young people.
4. Hourly output by workers _____ 1.3% in the first quarter because of the infectious disease.
5. Journalists on the whole don't create public opinion. They can help to _____ it.
6. He is _____ his time and energy on too many different things and therefore hasn't succeeded in any of them.
7. The academic year _____ at the beginning of October and ends at the end of December.
8. I _____ to the view that he is right and decide to support him.
9. Video is a good _____ for learning a foreign language.
10. What he said also _____ my account, so the headmaster believed me.
11. His efforts, the Duke _____ many years later, were distinctly half-hearted.
12. The exercise obviously will improve strength and _____.
13. He had no _____ evidence that anything extraordinary was happening. It was just his subjective inference.
14. But we begin to see that beneath that smug, arrogant _____ lies a fragile, vulnerable person, which I think is so often true of bullies.
15. Our tour prices bore little _____ to those in the holiday brochures.
16. Now let's return from this _____ to our subject, or our meeting will last too long.
17. Hold _____ to dreams, for when dreams go, life is but a barren field and frozen snow.
18. After a year she had _____ her ideal weight.
19. The clouds _____ as quickly as they had gathered.
20. In this cold climate, the climber climbed up the cliff with his _____ limbs. He almost couldn't feel them.

III. Translate the sentences into Chinese.

1. Even the tree itself has its proper time for putting forth shoots and blossoms, for growing, and for coming to maturity.
2. In middle age it is difficult, because the forces of the intellect are dissipated over a variety of objects and are not easily concentrated.

3. All the subjects that are to be learned should be arranged so as to suit the age of the students, that nothing which is beyond their comprehension should be given them to learn.
4. I maintain that a method can be found by means of which each person will be enabled to bring into his mental consciousness not only what he has learned, but more as well.
5. We do, it is true, make practical use of much that we have learned, but the amount that we recollect is unsatisfactory, and the fact remains that we are continually trying to pour water into a sieve.

Text 2

The Principles of Conciseness and Rapidity in Teaching

John Amos Comenius

1. "But these projects are too **wearisome**[1] and too **comprehensive**[2]," many readers will here **remark**[3]. "What a number of teachers and of libraries, and how much labour will be necessary in order that thorough instruction may be given in one subject!" I answer: this is undoubtedly so, and unless our labours are shortened, the task will be no easy one; for these are of ours in as long, as wide, and as deep as the universe that has to be **subdued**[4] by our minds. But who does not know that **diffuse**[5] and difficult things can be brought into a small **compass**[6]? Who is ignorant that weavers can **weave**[7] together a hundred thousand threads with the greatest rapidity, and can produce from these a great variety of stuffs? Or that millers can **grind**[8] thousands of grains with the greatest ease, and can separate the **bran**[9] from the flour with great exactness and without any difficulty? Everyone knows that engineers, without the slightest trouble and with comparatively small machines, can raise **enormous**[10] weights, and that a weight of one ounce, if at a sufficient distance from the **fulcrum**[11] of a **lever**[12], can **counterbalance**[13] many pounds. We see, therefore, that great achievements are more often a question of skill than of strength. Are learned men then to be the only people who do not know how to conduct their affairs with skill? Surely shame should compel us to **emulate**[14] the inventive spirit of other professions and find a remedy for the difficulties with which schools have **hitherto**[15] struggled.

2. It is impossible to find a remedy until we have discovered the diseases and their causes. What can it be that has **impeded**[16] the efforts of the schools and **hindered**[17] their success to such an extent that most men during their whole stay at school do not **traverse**[18] the whole range of the sciences and arts, while some of them scarcely even cross the threshold?

3. The causes of this are undoubtedly the following: firstly, no fixed landmarks were set up, which might serve as goals to be reached by the scholars at the end of each year, month, or day, and there was a complete lack of system.

4. Secondly, the roads that would **infallibly**[19] lead to these goals were not pointed out.

5. Thirdly, things that should naturally be associated were not joined together, but were kept apart.

6. Fourthly, the arts and the sciences were scarcely ever taught as part of an **encyclopedic**[20] whole, but were dealt out **piece-meal**[21]. This has been the reason why, in the eyes of the scholars, they seemed like a heap of wood or of **faggots**[22], in which the exact connection and combining-links can scarcely be discerned. Thus, it came to pass that some grasped one fact, others another, and that none received a really thorough and universal education.

7. Fifthly, many different methods were employed. Each school and even each teacher used a different one. What was worse, teachers would use one method in one subject or language, and another in another, and, worst of all, even in one individual subject they **varied**[23] their method, so that the scholar scarcely understood in what way he was expected to learn. This was the cause of the many delays that took place, and of the **lassitude**[24] of the scholar, who had frequently no desire even to attempt new branches of study.

8. Sixthly, no method was known by which instruction could be given to all the pupils in a class at the same time; the individual only was taught. With a large number of pupils this must have been an impossible task for the teacher. The pupils also must have found it very wearisome and extremely **irksome**[25], if each had to go on preparing work until his turn arrived.

9. Seventhly, if there were several teachers, this was a fresh source of confusion; since each hour some new subject was introduced. Not to mention the fact that a **diversity**[26] of teachers tends to **distract**[27] the mind quite as much as a diversity of books.

10. Finally, both in school and out of it, the scholars had perfect freedom **as regards**[28] the books they read, and the teachers gave them no **assistance**[29] in their choice. For all were **imbued**[30] with the idea that to read many authors **afforded**[31] many opportunities of making progress, whereas such diversity produced nothing but distraction. It was not surprising, therefore, that very

few mastered all the branches of study. The wonder was that any one was able to find his way out of such a **labyrinth**[32]—and indeed only the most gifted succeeded in doing so.

11. For the future, therefore, **hindrances**[33] and delays of this sort must be set aside, and we must make straight for our goal, neglecting everything that is not of immediate service.

12. In imitation of this

(ⅰ) There should only be one teacher in each school, or at any rate in each class.

(ⅱ) Only one author should be used for each subject studied.

(ⅲ) The same exercise should be given to the whole class.

(ⅳ) All subjects and languages should be taught by the same method.

(ⅴ) Everything should be taught thoroughly, briefly, and **pithily**[34], that the understanding may be, as it were, unlocked by one key, and may then **unravel**[35] fresh difficulties of its own accord.

(ⅵ) All things that are naturally connected ought to be taught in combination.

(ⅶ) Every subject should be taught in definitely graded steps, that the work of one day may thus expand that of the previous day, and lead up to that of the **morrow**[36].

(ⅷ) And finally, everything that is useless should be invariably **discarded**[37].

(From John Amos Comenius's *The Great Didactic*)

Vocabulary

1. **wearisome** /ˈwɪərisəm/
adj. very tiring and boring or frustrating 令人疲倦(或厌倦、沮丧)的
e. g. Sympathizing with him eventually becomes somewhat wearisome.

2. **comprehensive** /ˌkɒmprɪˈhensɪv/
adj. including everything that is needed or relevant 综合性的;全面的
e. g. The Rough Guide to Nepal is a comprehensive guide to the region.

3. **remark** /rɪˈmɑːk/
v. say 说;谈到
e. g. I remarked that I would go shopping that afternoon.

>>> Unit 4 Teaching and Learning Principles

4. subdue /səbˈdjuː/

v. defeat; bring under control by using force 征服;控制;压制;克制

e. g. He forced himself to subdue and overcome his fears.

5. diffuse /dɪˈfjuːs, dɪˈfjuːz/

adj. vague and difficult to understand or explain 分散的;含糊不清的;难以理解的

e. g. His writing is so diffuse and obscure that it is difficult to make out what it is he is trying to say.

6. compass /ˈkʌmpəs/

n. limits or abilities 界限;范围

e. g. Within the compass of a normal-sized book, such a comprehensive survey was not practicable.

7. weave /wiːv/

v. make by crossing threads over and under each other using a frame or machine called a loom 织;编织

8. grind /ɡraɪnd/

v. crush substance between two hard surfaces or with a machine until it becomes a fine powder 磨碎;碾碎;将……磨成粉

9. bran /bræn/

n. the outer skin of grain that is left when the grain has been used to make flour 麦麸;麸皮

10. enormous /ɪˈnɔːməs/

adj. to the great degree or extent（范围、程度）极大的

e. g. The problems facing the headmaster are enormous.

11. fulcrum /ˈfʊlkrəm/

n. the point on which a lever turns or is supported 支点;支柱

12. lever /ˈliːvə(r)/

n. a long bar, one end of which is placed under a heavy object so that when someone presses down on the other end they can move the object 杠杆;撬棒

13. counterbalance /ˌkaʊntəˈbæləns/

v. balance or correct things with something that has an equal but opposite effect 对……起平衡作用;抗衡;抵消

e. g. Add honey to counterbalance the acidity.

14. emulate /ˈemjuleɪt/

v. try to be like someone or something else, usually because you admire them （因为钦慕而）仿效;模仿

e. g. Sons are traditionally expected to emulate their fathers.

73

15. hitherto /ˌhɪðəˈtuː/

adv. until the present time 迄今；到目前为止

e. g. The polytechnics have hitherto been at an unfair disadvantage in competing for pupils and money.

16. impede /ɪmˈpiːd/

v. make their movement, development, or progress difficult 妨碍；阻碍；阻止

e. g. Fallen rock is impeding the progress of rescue workers.

17. hinder /ˈhɪndə(r)/

v. make it more difficult to do something or make progress; make it difficult to move forward or move around 阻碍；妨碍；阻止；牵制；束缚（动作）

e. g. Does the fact that your players are part-timers help or hinder you? Let me know it, please.

Landslides and bad weather are continuing to hinder the arrival of relief supplies to the area.

18. traverse /trəˈvɜːs, ˈtrævɜːs/

v. go across 横穿；横越；穿过

e. g. I traversed the narrow pedestrian bridge.

19. infallibly /ɪnˈfæləbli/

adv. without making mistakes 绝对无误地

20. encyclopedic /ɪnˌsaɪkləˈpiːdɪk/

adj. very full, complete, and thorough in the amount of knowledge or information that it has 百科全书般的；知识丰富的

e. g. She has an encyclopedic knowledge of natural history.

21. piece-meal /ˈpiːsmiːl/

adv. happening gradually, usually at irregular intervals, and probably not satisfactory 逐渐发生的；零敲碎打的；零散的

e. g. Our parents started selling off the family farm piecemeal several years ago, and now there are only five acres left.

22. faggot /ˈfæɡət/

n. a bundle of sticks and branches bound together 柴把

23. vary /ˈveəri/

v. change from one condition, form, or state to another; make (something) different （使）变化

e. g. The cost of a room at the hotel varies with the season.
　　I try to vary my diet by eating different kinds of foods.

24. lassitude /ˈlæsɪtjuːd/

n. a state of tiredness, laziness, or lack of interest 无力；困乏；倦怠

e. g. Symptoms of anaemia include general fatigue and lassitude.

25. irksome /ˈɜːksəm/

adj. irritating or annoying 令人恼怒的；令人厌烦的

e.g. I don't like the irksome task of cleaning up.

26. diversity /daɪˈvɜːsəti/

n. the state of containing many different elements 多样性；多样化

e.g. The island has more diversity in plant life than other islands.

27. distract /dɪˈstrækt/

v. take attention away from 分散（注意力）；使分心

e.g. The students are easily distracted, especially when they are tired.

28. as regards

with regard to; concerning 关于

e.g. I have little information as regards her fitness for the post.

29. assistance /əˈsɪstəns/

n. help given to someone or help that allows something to be done 帮助；协助

e.g. I'll be happy to provide you with whatever assistance you may need.

30. imbue /ɪmˈbjuː/

v. become filled with something 向……灌输；使充满

e.g. As you listen, you notice how every single word is imbued with a breathless sense of wonder.

31. afford /əˈfɔːd/

v. give something 提供；给予

e.g. This affords us the opportunity to ask questions about how the systems might change.

32. labyrinth /ˈlæbərɪnθ/

n. a complicated series of paths or passages, through which it is difficult to find one's way 迷宫；迷阵

33. hindrance /ˈhɪndrəns/

n. the act of hindering someone or something 阻碍；妨碍

e.g. They boarded their flight to Paris without hindrance.

34. pithily /ˈpɪθɪli/

adv. in a short and direct way 简洁扼要地；言简意赅地

e.g. The essay was pithily written.

35. unravel /ʌnˈrævl/

v. make something become clearer 揭开；揭示

e.g. Gradually, with an intelligent use of flashbacks, Yves' story unravels.

36. morrow /ˈmɒrəʊ/

n. the next day or tomorrow 翌日；次日

37. discard /dɪˈskɑːd/

v. get rid of something because someone no longer wants it or needs it 丢弃；抛弃

e. g. Read the manufacturer's guidelines before discarding the box.

Exercises for Text 2

I. Decide whether the statements are true (T) or false (F) according to the text.

1. There should only be one teacher in each school, and he should teach his students at the same rate.
2. Different students should use different books that fit their needs.
3. Students should have freedom to choose the book they read.
4. Different exercises should be designed for the students in the same class according to their level.
5. Teachers need to adopt different methods for students of different character traits.

II. Translate the following sentences with the key words in the parentheses.

1. 房间里到处都是乱扔的报纸。(discard)
2. 一位年轻的母亲飞抵冰岛，要揭开丈夫失踪之谜。(unravel)
3. 他满怀寻求社会正义的愿望。(imbue)
4. 不要同她讲话，因为她的注意力很容易分散。(distract)
5. 案件卷宗全部丢失，致使进一步的调查受阻。(hinder)
6. 坠落的石头阻滞了救援人员的救援进程。(impede)
7. 她希望在运动成绩方面赶上姐姐。(emulate)
8. 他谈论到农村的兴旺景象。(remark)
9. 这项计划给年轻人提供了获得工作经验的机会。(afford)
10. 到目前为止，我们还没有成功。(hitherto)

III. Explain the following sentences in your own words.

1. But who does not know that diffuse and difficult things can be brought into a small compass?
2. We see, therefore, that great achievements are more often a question of skill than of strength.
3. No fixed landmarks were set up, which might serve as goals to be reached by the scholars at the end of each year, month, or day, and there was a complete lack of system.
4. The arts and the sciences were scarcely ever taught as part of an encyclopedic whole, but were dealt out piece-meal.
5. This was the cause of many delays that took place, and of the lassitude of the scholar, who had frequently no desire even to attempt new branches of study.

>>> Unit 4 Teaching and Learning Principles

Learning Strategies

Searching Information by Using the Internet

When we want to understand a difficult text, sometimes we need to search information related to the text. The Internet is a useful place for us to get information. For example, if we want to find more articles about the principle of teaching, the following free resource website can be used:

http://gen.lib.rus.ec/

http://www.gutenberg.org/

https://ebookee.org/

https://www.planetebook.com/

https://www.hathitrust.org/HathiTrust

https://en.wikibooks.org/wiki/Main_PageWikibooks

https://www.getfreeebooks.com/

http://www.onlinefreebooks.net

Now you can surf the Internet to find and summarize the principles of teaching according to students' individuality.

Unit Project

Work in groups to make research on articles about the principle of education and have a debate about the principles.

1. Find articles about the principle of education and sum up their views.
2. Hold a discussion in groups about whether you agree with the views of those articles.
3. Give an analysis of those articles by comparing Comenius's view and their views.
4. Choose the most controversial principle and have a debate about it.

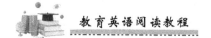

Unit 5

Respecting Children

Pre-reading questions:

1. What are John Locke and Jean Jacques Rousseau's ideas about how to educate children?
2. What's the influence of their ideas on humanism?

>>> Unit 5 Respecting Children

Text 1
Some Thoughts Concerning Education

John Locke

1. **Reasoning**—It will perhaps be wondered, that I mention reasoning with children, and yet I cannot but think that is the true way of dealing with them. They understand it as early as they do language; and, if I misobserve not, they love to be treated as rational creatures, sooner than is imagined …

2. But when I talk of reasoning, I do not intend any other, but such as is suited to the child's capacity and **apprehension**[1]. Nobody can think a boy of three or seven years old should be argued with as a grown man. Long discourses, and philosophical reasonings, at best, amaze and confound, but do not instruct children. When I say therefore that they must be treated as rational creatures, I mean that you should make them sensible, by the mildness of your **carriage**[2], and the **composure**[3], even in your correction of them, that what you do is reasonable in you, and useful and necessary for them; and that it is not out of **caprice**[4], passion, or fancy, that you command or forbid them anything. This they are capable of understanding; and there is no virtue they should be excited to, nor fault they should be kept from, which I do not think they may be convinced of, but it must be by such reasons as their age and understanding are capable of, and those proposed always in very few and plain words. The foundations on which several duties are built, and the fountains of right and wrong, from which they spring, are not, perhaps, easily to be let into the minds of grown men, not used to abstract their thoughts from common received opinions. Much less are children capable of reasonings from remote principles. They cannot conceive the force of long deductions: the reasons that move them must be obvious, and **level**[5] to their thoughts, and such as may (if I may so say) be felt and touched …

3. **Examples**—But of all the ways whereby children are to be instructed, and their manners formed, the plainest, easiest, and most **efficacious**[6] is,

to set before their eyes the examples of those things you would have them do, or avoid; which, when they are pointed out to them, in the practice of persons within their knowledge, with some reflections on their beauty and **unbecomingness**[7], are of more force to draw or deter their imitation, than any discourses which can be made to them. Virtues and vices can by no words be so plainly set before their understandings as the actions of other men will shew them, when you direct their observation, and bid them view this or that good or bad quality in their practice. And the beauty or **uncomeliness**[8] of many things, in good and ill breeding, will be better learnt, and make deeper impressions on them, in the examples of others, than from any rules or instructions that can be given about them.

4. **Curiosity**—Curiosity in children is but an appetite after knowledge, and therefore ought to be encouraged in them, not only as a good sign, but as the great instrument nature has provided to remove that ignorance they were born with, and which, without this busy inquisitiveness, will make them dull and useless creatures. The ways to encourage it, and keep it active and vigorous, are, I suppose, these following:

5. Not to **check**[9] or **discountenance**[10] any inquiries he shall make, nor suffer them to be laughed at; but to answer all his questions, and explain the matters he desires to know, so as to make them as much intelligible to him as suits the capacity of his age and knowledge. But confound not his understanding with **explications**[11] or notions that are above it, or with the variety or number of things that are not to his present purpose. Mark what it is his mind aims at in the question, and not what words he expresses it in; and, when you have informed and satisfied him in that, you shall see how his thoughts will proceed on to other things, and how by fit answers to his inquiries he may be led on farther than perhaps you could imagine. For knowledge to the understanding is acceptable as light to the eyes, and children are pleased and delighted with it exceedingly, especially if they see that their inquiries are regarded, and that their desire of knowing is encouraged and **commended**[12]. And I doubt not, but one great reason why many children abandon themselves wholly to silly sports, and **trifle**[13] away all their time in trifling, is, because they have found their curiosity **balked**[14], and their inquiries neglected. But had they been treated with more kindness and respect, and their questions answered, as they should, to their satisfaction,

I doubt not but they would have taken more pleasure in learning, and improving their knowledge, **wherein**[15] there would be still newness and variety, which is what they are delighted with, than in returning over and over to the same play and playthings.

6. To this serious answering their questions, and informing their understandings in what they desire, as if it were a matter that needed it, should be added some peculiar ways of **commendation**[16]. Let others, whom they esteem, be told before their faces of the knowledge they have in such and such things; and since we are all, even from our cradles, vain and proud creatures, let their vanity be flattered with things that will do them good, and let their pride set them on work on something which may turn to their advantage. Upon this ground, you shall find that there cannot be a greater **spur**[17] to the attaining what you would have the eldest learn and know himself, than to set him upon teaching it to his younger brothers and sisters.

7. As children's inquiries are not to be **slighted**[18], so also great care is to be taken that they never receive deceitful and **eluding**[19] answers. They easily perceive when they are slighted or deceived, and quickly learn the trick of neglect, **dissimulation**[20] and falsehood, which they observe others to make use of. We are not to **entrench**[21] upon truth in any conversation, but least of all with children; since, if we play false with them, we not only deceive their expectation, and hinder their knowledge, but corrupt their innocence, and teach them the worst of vices. They are travellers who newly arrived in a strange country, of which they know nothing. We should therefore make **conscience**[22] not to mislead them. And though their questions seem sometimes not very **material**[23], yet they should be seriously answered; for however they may appear to us (to whom they are long since known) inquiries not worth the making, they are of moment to those who are wholly ignorant. Children are strangers to all we are acquainted with; and all the things they meet with are at first unknown to them, as they once were to us, and happy are they who meet with **civil**[24] people that will **comply**[25] with their ignorance, and help them to get out of it. If you or I now should be set down in Japan, with all our **prudence**[26] and knowledge about us, a **conceit**[27] **whereof**[28] makes us perhaps so apt to slight the thoughts and inquiries of children; should we, I say, be set down in Japan, we should, no doubt (if we would inform ourselves of what

is there to be known), ask a thousand questions, which, to a **supercilious**[29] or **inconsiderate**[30] Japanner, would seem very idle and **impertinent**[31]; and yet to us would be natural; and we should be glad to find a man so kind and **humane**[32] as to answer them and instruct our ignorance. When any new thing comes in their way, children usually ask the common question of a stranger, "What is it?" whereby they ordinarily mean nothing but the name; and therefore, to tell them how it is called, is usually the proper answer to that demand. The next question usually is "What is it for?" And to this it should be answered truly and directly: the use of the thing should be told, and the way explained, how it serves to such a purpose, as far as their capacities can comprehend it; and so of any other circumstances they shall ask about it; not turning them going till you have given them all the satisfaction they are capable of, and so leading them by your answers into farther questions. And perhaps, to a grown man, such conversation will not be altogether so idle and insignificant as we are apt to imagine. The native and untaught suggestions of **inquisitive**[33] children do often offer things that may set a considering man's thoughts on work. And I think there is frequently more to be learned from the unexpected questions of a child, than the discourses of men, who talk in a road, according to the notions they have borrowed, and the prejudices of their education.

8. Perhaps it may not sometimes be **amiss**[34] to excite their curiosity, by bringing strange and new things in their way, on purpose to **engage**[35] their inquiry, and give them occasion to inform themselves about them; and if by chance their curiosity leads them to ask what they should not know, it is a great deal better to tell them plainly that it is a thing that belongs not to them to know, than to **pop them off**[36] with a falsehood or a **frivolous**[37] answer.

(From John Locke's *Some Thoughts Concerning Education*)

Vocabulary

1. **apprehension** /ˌæprɪˈhenʃn/
   n. understanding 理解
   e. g. He has an overall apprehension of the present international situation.

2. **carriage** /ˈkærɪdʒ/

n. the way someone moves their body when they are walking 仪态

e. g. She has an elegant carriage.

3. **composure** /kəmˈpəʊʒə(r)/

n. the feeling of being calm, confident, and relaxed 镇静

e. g. He made her laugh so much that she had to stop and regain her composure several times.

4. **caprice** /kəˈpriːs/

n. a sudden and unexpected change of opinion or behavior without any good reason 反复无常;善变;任性

e. g. I lived in terror of her sudden caprices and moods.

5. **level** /ˈlevl/

adj. at the same height 等高的;地位相同的

6. **efficacious** /ˌefɪˈkeɪʃəs/

adj. producing the effect that you intended 有效的

e. g. The nasal spray was new on the market and highly efficacious.

7. **unbecomingness** /ˌʌnbɪˈkʌmɪŋnɪs/

n. the state of not being beautiful and appropriate 不好看;不合适

8. **uncomeliness** /ˌʌnˈkʌmlɪnɪs/

n. the state of not being in keeping with accepted standards of what is right or proper in polite society 精致;不恰当

9. **check** /tʃek/

v. hold back 抑制

e. g. She started to speak but then checked herself.

10. **discountenance** /dɪsˈkaʊntməns/

v. look with disfavor on 不赞成

11. **explication** /ˌeksplɪˈkeɪʃn/

n. a detailed explanation of the meaning of something 说明

e. g. McKen criticises the lack of explication of what the term "areas" means.

12. **commend** /kəˈmend/

v. express a good opinion of 赞扬

e. g. The general commended the sergeant for his bravery.

13. **trifle** /ˈtraɪfl/

v. waste time; spend one's time idly or inefficiently 虚度

e. g. Don't trifle away your time and your money.

14. **balk** /bɔːk/

v. refuse to comply 阻碍

e. g. He balks at sending his children to expensive private schools.

15. wherein /weər'ɪn/

adv. in which; where 在哪方面

e. g. This was a riding school wherein we could learn the art of horsemanship.

16. commendation /ˌkɒmen'deɪʃn/

n. the act of expressing a good opinion 赞扬

e. g. We have heard lots of commendation for his bravery.

17. spur /spɜː(r)/

n. a verbalization that encourages you to attempt something 激励

e. g. Suddenly, I understood that having obligations can act as a spur and a discipline.

18. slight /slaɪt/

v. pay no attention to; disrespect 轻视

e. g. His suggestion was slighted over by his parents.

19. elude /i'luːd/

v. escape, either physically or mentally 逃避

e. g. The two men managed to elude the police for six weeks.

20. dissimulation /dɪˌsɪmjuˈleɪʃn/

n. the act of deceiving 掩饰;装糊涂

21. entrench /ɪn'trentʃ/

v. impinge or infringe upon 妨碍

22. conscience /'kɒnʃəns/

n. conformity to one's own sense of right conduct 良知

e. g. Could you live with that on your conscience?

23. material /mə'tɪəriəl/

adj. important 重要的

e. g. She omitted information that was material to the case.

24. civil /'sɪvl/

adj. not rude; marked by satisfactory (or especially minimal) adherence to social usages and sufficient but not noteworthy consideration for others 礼貌的;客气的

e. g. It's civil of you to say so.

25. comply /kəm'plaɪ/

v. act in accordance with someone's rules, commands, or wishes 顺应;顺从

e. g. They refused to comply with the UN resolution.

26. prudence /'pruːdns/

n. discretion in practical affairs 谨慎

e. g. Britain has warned travellers to exercise prudence and care.

27. conceit /kən'siːt/

n. feelings of excessive pride 自负;骄傲自大

e. g. He knew, without conceit, that he was considered a genius.

28. **whereof** /weər'ɒv/

adv. of what 关于那个

e. g. They were the earliest poets whereof there is record.

29. **supercilious** /ˌsuːpə'sɪliəs/

adj. behaving towards other people as if you think you are better than they are 高傲的;傲慢的

e. g. Her eyebrows were arched in supercilious surprise.

30. **inconsiderate** /ˌɪnkən'sɪdərət/

adj. lacking regard for the rights or feelings of others 不为他人着想的

e. g. Motorists were criticised for being inconsiderate to pedestrians.

31. **impertinent** /ɪm'pɜːtmənt/

adj. improperly forward or bold 无礼的

e. g. Would it be impertinent to ask why you are leaving?

32. **humane** /hjuː'meɪn/

adj. showing evidence of moral and intellectual advancement 人道的;仁爱的

e. g. They supported the humane killing of animals.

33. **inquisitive** /ɪn'kwɪzətɪv/

adj. showing curiosity 好问的;好奇的

e. g. I hope you do not think I am inquisitive, but who's fired?

34. **amiss** /ə'mɪs/

adj. not functioning properly 出了差错的

e. g. She sensed something was amiss and called the police.

35. **engage** /ɪn'geɪdʒ/

v. attract and keep someone's interest or attention 吸引

e. g. They never learned skills to engage the attention of the others.

36. **pop off**

leave quickly (使)突然离开

e. g. She should pop off back to Scotland.

37. **frivolous** /'frɪvələs/

adj. not serious in content or attitude or behavior 轻率的

e. g. I was a bit too frivolous to be a doctor.

Exercises for Text 1

I. Read the text and answer the questions.

1. What is the best way to reason with children?
2. What's the best way to teach children manners?

3. What will happen to children when they lack curiosity?
4. What are the ways to keep children's curiosity?
5. What are the implications of Locke's view on curiosity in modern education?

II. Complete the sentences with the words below. Change the form where necessary.

check	efficacious	caprice	composure	carriage
commend	spur	conscience	conceit	humane
trifle	slight	prudence	supercilious	frivolous
wherein	elude	comply	impertinent	engage

1. Her figure was slim and fragile, and in spite of her humble dress, she had something of the grace and _____ of a gentlewoman.
2. Collins, and whatever might be his feelings toward her friend, met her with every appearance of _____.
3. Don't act on _____. Study your problem.
4. They hope the new drug will prove especially _____ in the relief of pain.
5. The headmaster is determined to _____ the growth of spending in school to cope with the financial crisis.
6. She was _____ on her handling of the situation. She showed her courage and wisdom.
7. I _____ my life away on worldly desires. How I regret about this!
8. Adequate housing is possible in developed, mixed economies _____ the interests of the poor have prevailed.
9. Creating content for new platforms has been a(n) _____ to innovation and a fresh approach.
10. They felt _____ by not being adequately consulted.
11. Love is a butterfly. The more you chase it, the more it _____ you.
12. I'll write and apologize. I've had it on my _____ for weeks.
13. A lack of _____ may lead to financial problems, so we need to be more careful with our money.
14. The commander said that the army would _____ with the ceasefire.
15. Error is often the precursor of what is correct, but _____ is the prelude to a fall.
16. His high rank did not render him _____; on the contrary, he was all attention to everybody.
17. Would it be _____ to ask where exactly you were?
18. In the mid-nineteenth century, Dorothea Dix began to campaign for _____ treatment of the mentally ill.

19. The introduction should immediately _____ attention, good will and respect, as well as lead to the subject matter.
20. That is not a(n) _____ answer, but a serious one.

III. Translate the sentences into Chinese.

1. And there is no virtue they should be excited to, nor fault they should be kept from, which I do not think they may be convinced of, but it must be by such reasons as their age and understanding are capable of, and those proposed always in very few and plain words.
2. They would have taken more pleasure in learning, and improving their knowledge, wherein there would be still newness and variety, which is what they are delighted with, than in returning over and over to the same play and playthings.
3. Let their vanity be flattered with things that will do them good, and let their pride set them on work on something which may turn to their advantage.
4. There cannot be a greater spur to the attaining what you would have the eldest learn and know himself, than to set him upon teaching it to his younger brothers and sisters.
5. Children are strangers to all we are acquainted with; and all the things they meet with, are at first unknown to them, as they once were to us.

Text 2

Emile, or on Education

Jean Jacques Rousseau

1. God makes all things good; man **meddles**[1] with them and they become evil. He forces one soil to **yield**[2] the products of another, one tree to bear another's fruit. He confuses and **confounds**[3] time, place, and natural conditions. He **mutilates**[4] his dog, his horse, and his slave. He destroys and **defaces**[5] all things; he loves all that is **deformed**[6] and monstrous; he will have nothing as nature made it, not even man himself, who must learn his paces like a saddle-horse, and be shaped to his master's taste like the trees in his garden.

2. Yet things would be worse without this education, and mankind cannot be made by halves. Under existing conditions, a man left to himself from birth would be **more of**[7] a monster than the rest. Prejudice, authority, necessity, example, all the social conditions into which we are **plunged**[8], would **stifle**[9] nature in him and put nothing in her place. She would be like a **sapling**[10] chance **sown**[11] in the midst of the highway, bent hither and **thither**[12] and soon **crushed**[13] by the passers-by.

3. Tender, anxious mother, I **appeal**[14] to you. You can remove this young tree from the highway and **shield**[15] it from the crushing force of social conventions. Tend and water it **ere**[16] it dies. One day its fruit will reward your care. From the **outset**[17] raise a wall round your child's soul; another may sketch the plan; you alone should carry it in to **execution**[18].

4. Plants are fashioned by cultivation, man by education. If a man were born tall and strong, his size and strength would be of no good to him till he had learnt to use them; they would even harm him by preventing others from coming to his aid; left to himself he would die of **want**[19] before he knew his needs. We **lament**[20] the helplessness of infancy; we fail to perceive that the race would have perished had not man begun by being a child.

5. We are born weak, we need strength; helpless, we need aid; foolish, we need reason. All that we lack at birth, all that we need when we come to man's estate, is the gift of education. This education comes to us from nature, from men, or from things. The inner growth of our organs and faculties is the education of nature, the use we learn to make of this growth is the education of men, what we gain by our experience of our surroundings is the education of things.

6. Thus we are each taught by three masters. If their teaching conflicts, the scholar is ill-educated and will never be at peace with himself; if their teaching agrees, he goes straight to his goal, he lives at peace with himself, he is well-educated.

7. Now of these three factors in education nature is wholly beyond our control, things are only partly in our power; the education of men is the only one controlled by us; and even here our power is largely **illusory**[21] for who can hope to direct every word and deed of all with whom the child has to do.

8. Viewed as an art, the success of education is almost impossible, since the essential conditions of success are beyond our control. Our efforts may bring us within sight of the goal, but fortune must favour us if we are to reach it.

9. What is this goal? As we have just shown, it is the goal of nature. Since all three modes of education must work together, the two that we can control must follow the lead of that which is beyond our control.

10. Our inner conflicts are caused by these **contradictions**[22]. Drawn this way by nature and that way by man, compelled to yield to both forces, we make a **compromise**[23] and reach neither goal. We go through life, struggling and hesitating, and die before we have found peace, useless alike to ourselves and to others.

11. There remains the education of the home or of nature; but how will a man live with others if he is educated for himself alone? If the twofold aims could be resolved into one by removing the man's self-contradictions, one great obstacle to his happiness would be gone. To judge this, you must see the man full-grown; you must have noted his inclinations, watched his progress, followed his steps; in a word you must really know a natural man. When you have read this work, I think you will have made some progress in this inquiry.

12. In the social order where each has his own place a man must be educated for it. If such a one leaves his own station, he is fit for nothing else.

His education is only useful when fate agrees with his parents' choice; if not, education harms the scholar, if only by the prejudices it has created.

13. In the natural order men are all equal and their common calling is that of manhood, so that a well-educated man cannot fail to do well in that calling and those related to it. It matters little to me whether my pupil is intended for the army, the church, or the law. Before his parents chose a calling for him nature called him to be a man. Life is the trade I would teach him. When he leaves me, I grant you, he will be neither a **magistrate**[24], a soldier, nor a priest; he will be a man. All that becomes a man he will learn as quickly as another. **In vain**[25] ill fate changes his station, he will always be in his right place. The real object of our study is man and his environment. To my mind those of us who can best endure the good and evil of life are the best educated; hence it follows that true education consists less in **precept**[26] than in practice. We begin to learn when we begin to live; our education begins with ourselves, our first teacher is our nurse. The ancients used the word Education in a different sense, it meant Nurture. Thus, education, discipline, and instruction are three things as different in their purpose as the dame, the **usher**[27], and the teacher. But these distinctions are undesirable and the child should only follow one guide.

14. People think only of preserving their child's life; this is not enough, he must be taught to preserve his own life when he is a man, to bear the **buffets**[28] of fortune, to **brave**[29] wealth and poverty, to live at need among the snows of Iceland or on the **scorching**[30] rocks of Malta. In vain you guard against death; he must die; and even if you do not kill him with your precautions, they are mistaken. Teach him to live rather than to avoid death: life is not breath, but action, the use of our senses, our mind, our faculties, every part of ourselves which make us conscious of our being. Life consists less in length of days than in the keen sense of living. A man may be buried at a hundred and may never have lived at all. He would have **fared**[31] better had he died young.

15. Our wisdom is slavish prejudice, our customs consist in control, **constraint**[32], **compulsion**[33]. Civilized man is born and dies a slave. The infant is bound up in **swaddling**[34] clothes, the corpse is nailed down in his coffin. All his life long man is imprisoned by our **institutions**[35].

(From Jean Jacques Rousseau's *Emile, or on Education*)

Vocabulary

1. meddle /ˈmedl/

v. try to influence or change something without being asked 管闲事；干涉

e.g. He had no right to meddle in her affairs.

2. yield /jiːld/

v. produce 出产（作物）；产（肉）

3. confound /kənˈfaʊnd/

v. make someone feel surprised or confused 使困惑；使惊讶

e.g. She confounded her critics and proved she could do the job.

4. mutilate /ˈmjuːtɪleɪt/

v. severely damage 使残缺不全；使受到严重损伤

e.g. More than 30 horses have been mutilated in the last nine months.

5. deface /dɪˈfeɪs/

v. spoil something by writing or drawing things on it 损伤……的外观；在……上乱涂乱画

e.g. It's illegal to deface banknotes.

6. deform /dɪˈfɔːm/

v. cause something to have an unnatural shape （使）变形；（使）成畸形

e.g. The disease eventually deforms the bones.

7. much of

quite good 比较好的

e.g. He is not much of an artist. His works are of low quality.

8. plunge /plʌndʒ/

v. push something quickly or violently into 将……投入；将……插入；将……刺进

e.g. A soldier plunged a bayonet into his body.

9. stifle /ˈstaɪfl/

v. prevent something from continuing 扼杀；压制；抑止

e.g. Regulations on children stifled creativity.

10. sapling /ˈsæplɪŋ/

n. a young tree 幼树

11. sown /səʊn/

v. the past form of sow 播种；种

12. thither /ˈðɪðə(r)/

adv. to the place that has already been mentioned 到那里；向那边

e.g. They have dragged themselves thither for shelter.

13. crush /krʌʃ/

v. push or press 推；压；挤

e. g. Unfortunately some of the flowers got crushed when we were moving them.

14. appeal /əˈpiːl/

v. make a serious and urgent request 呼吁；恳请；恳求

e. g. The headmaster appealed to the students to stay calm.

15. shield /ʃiːld/

v. protect someone from something 保护；掩护；庇护

e. g. I think she's shielded her child from the real world for too long.

16. ere /eə/

conj. before 在……之前

e. g. It was not long ere a call came from the house and recalled me from my reflections.

17. outset /ˈaʊtset/

n. beginning 开始

e. g. You need to decide at the outset what kind of learning programme you want to follow.

18. execution /ˌeksɪˈkjuːʃn/

n. the act of carrying out 执行；实施

e. g. We put the plan into execution.

19. want /wɒnt/

n. lack 缺乏；缺少

e. g. He was disliked for his want of manners and charm.

20. lament /ləˈment/

v. express sadness, regret, or disappointment about 为……悲痛；哀叹；痛惜

21. illusory /ɪˈluːsəri/

adj. false or impossible 幻觉的；虚假的；不切实际的

e. g. His freedom is illusory.

22. contradiction /ˌkɒntrəˈdɪkʃn/

n. the state of being completely different from other aspects, and so making the situation confused or difficult to understand 矛盾；不一致

e. g. There is a contradiction between the two sets of figures.

23. compromise /ˈkɒmprəmaɪz/

n. a situation in which people accept something slightly different from what they really want, because of circumstances or because they are considering the wishes of other people 折中；妥协；让步

e. g. Encourage your child to reach a compromise between what he wants and what you want.

24. **magistrate** /ˈmædʒɪstreɪt/

n. local official 地方官员；法官

25. **in vain**

not successfully in attempt 徒然地；枉然地

e.g. He tried in vain to stop her.

26. **precept** /ˈpriːsept/

n. a general rule that helps someone to decide how they should behave in particular circumstances 准则；规范；戒律

e.g. Feminism is based on the precept that men and women should be equal.

27. **usher** /ˈʌʃə(r)/

n. a person who shows people where to sit, for example at a wedding or at a concert（婚礼、音乐会等的）引座员；招待员；迎宾员

28. **buffet** /ˈbʊfeɪ, bəˈfeɪ/

n. blow 打击

29. **brave** /breɪv/

v. deliberately expose oneself to difficulties, usually in order to achieve something（通常为达到某目标）勇敢面对

e.g. Thousands have braved icy rain to show their support.

30. **scorching** /ˈskɔːtʃɪŋ/

adj. very hot; very fierce 灼热的；激烈的

e.g. Several days of scorching heat made this summer unbearable.

31. **fare** /feə(r)/

v. achieve certain degree of success in a particular situation or activity 进展；进行

e.g. It is unlikely that the marine industry will fare any better in September.

32. **constraint** /kənˈstreɪnt/

n. control over the way someone behaves 克制

33. **compulsion** /kəmˈpʌlʃn/

n. the act of forcing someone to do something 强迫；强制

e.g. Many universities argued that students learned more when they were in classes out of choice rather than compulsion.

34. **swaddle** /ˈswɒdl/

v. wrap little baby; limit 用襁褓包裹婴儿；束缚；限制

35. **institution** /ˌɪnstɪˈtjuːʃn/

n. a custom or system that is considered an important or typical feature of a particular society or group, usually because it has existed for a long time 习俗；制度

e.g. I believe in the institution of marriage.

Exercises for Text 2

I. Decide whether the statements are true (T) or false (F) according to the text.

1. Rousseau thinks men meddle with nature and therefore, they become evil.
2. The helplessness of infants are useless at all. It only shows they are very weak.
3. Well-educated people can live at peace with themselves.
4. Our inner conflicts are caused by these contradictions between nature and the feature of man.
5. Human beings have been constrained since they are a little child.

II. Translate the following sentences with the key words in the parentheses.

1. 已经有人在问科学家是否有权干预这类事情。(meddle)
2. 他的选择可能会让我们所有人感到困惑。(confound)
3. 她把脸扎进一盆凉水里。(plunge)
4. 他们希望新规则不会压制创意。(stifle)
5. 警方呼吁证人挺身而出。(appeal)
6. 他用一只旧口袋挡住头顶的阳光。(shield)
7. 他未能履行职责,所以被解雇了。(execution)
8. 他从一开始就很信任我这个老朋友的儿子。(outset)
9. 由于缺乏休息,这些人日渐虚弱。(want)
10. 学校没有强求学生上课。(compulsion)

III. Explain the following sentences in your own words.

1. He will have nothing as nature made it, not even man himself, who must learn his paces like a saddle-horse, and be shaped to his master's taste like the trees in his garden.
2. Prejudice, authority, necessity, example, all the social conditions into which we are plunged, would stifle nature in him and put nothing in her place.
3. Life is the trade I would teach him. When he leaves me, I grant you, he will be neither a magistrate, a soldier, nor a priest; he will be a man.
4. Teach him to live rather than to avoid death: life is not breath, but action, the use of our senses, our mind, our faculties, every part of ourselves which make us conscious of our being.
5. A man may be buried at a hundred and may never have lived at all. He would have fared better had he died young.

Learning Strategies

Remembering Words by Vocabulary Clouds

Vocabulary clouds can help us remember new words more quickly.
1. We need to put the words into different groups, for example, "unbecomingness, uncomeliness, ill breeding" in the first text can be put in the group which is used to describe a person's bad manners.
2. Write down the words on the clouds.
3. Draw picture of the vocabulary clouds to help us remember their meanings if necessary. For example,

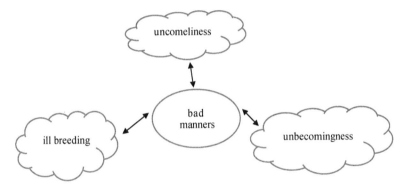

Now you can draw vocabulary clouds for those words expressing respect for children's nature.

Unit Project

Work in groups to make research on articles about the way to respect children's nature and write an essay about it.
1. Find articles related to respecting children's nature and sum up their views.
2. Hold a discussion in groups about whether you agree with the views of those articles.
3. Give an analysis of those articles by using the two authors' views.
4. Write an essay of 800 words about it.

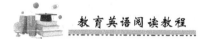

Unit 6

Steps in Instruction or Thinking

Pre-reading questions:

1. What do you know about Herbart's four steps in instruction?
2. What do you know about John Dewey's five steps in thinking?
3. What steps do you think we should follow in teaching?

>>> Unit 6   Steps in Instruction or Thinking

Text 1

Steps in Instruction

Johann Friedrich Herbart

1. What things must take place **consecutively**¹ and one through the other, and what on the contrary must do so **contemporaneously**², and each with its proper and original power—are questions which touch all employments and all plans in which a great number of complicated measures have to be carried out. For a beginning is always made at the same time from several sides, and much always must be prepared by what had gone before. These are **as it were**³ the two **dimensions**⁴, conformably to which we have to guide our steps.

2. Our preceding concepts show us that instruction has to develop knowledge and sympathy at the same time, as **diverse**⁵ and fundamentally individual states of mind. If we look at the subordinate parts, there is clearly a certain **succession**⁶ and dependence, but nevertheless no strict sequence. Speculation and taste doubtless **presuppose**⁷ the comprehension of the **empirical**⁸; but while this comprehension always goes forward, they do not perhaps wait for its end. Indeed, they rather become active **betimes**⁹, and develop themselves **thenceforward**¹⁰ parallel with the **expansion**¹¹ of mere knowledge of the **manifold**¹², and follow everywhere at its heels if no **impediment**¹³ **intervene**¹⁴. Especially remarkable is speculative activity during the period when children perpetually ask—Why? Taste hides itself perhaps more amongst other movements of attention and sympathy, yet it always supplies its **quota**¹⁵ to the preferences and dislikes by which children show their distinction of things. And how much more rapidly would it develop were we to present to it at first the simplest relationships, and not throw it at once into incomprehensible **complications**¹⁶. Since taste as well as **meditation**¹⁷ is something original which cannot be learned, we ought, independently of experience, to expect that in the **sphere**¹⁸ of sufficiently known objects,

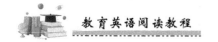

both must become active without delay, if the mind be not otherwise distracted or oppressed. It is a matter of course that teachers to perceive what is moving in the children's minds must themselves possess that same culture, the most **subtle**[19] traces of which they have to observe in them. This is just the misfortune of education, that so many **feeble**[20] lights which **glimmer**[21] in tender youth, are long since completely **extinguished**[22] in adults, who are therefore unfitted to **kindle**[23] those feeble lights into flame.

3. The preceding is also true of the parts of sympathy. Among a small group of children, if only a little sympathy exists and is kept awake, a certain need of social order for the common good develops itself spontaneously. And as the most **barbarous**[24] nations are not without **divinities**[25], so the souls of children have a **presentiment**[26] of an unseen power, which can **exercise**[27] influence in some way or other in the sphere of their wishes. **Whence**[28] else comes the facility with which various kinds both of superstitious and genuinely religious ideas obtain entrance into, and influence with, the little ones? For a child, however, who finds itself in close dependence on its parents and guardians, these visible persons certainly occupy the place which the feeling of dependence assigns to the unseen powers, and just for this reason, the earliest religious instruction is only an exceedingly simple expansion of the relation of the parents to the children, as in the same way the first social ideas will be taken from the family.

4. The varieties of interest then which instruction ought to cultivate, present to us only differences in things simultaneously, but not a distinct succession of steps.

5. On the other hand, the formal fundamental concepts developed in the beginning are based on the **antitheses**[29] between things which follow one upon another.

6. Concentration, above all, ought to precede reflection, but at what distance? This question remains generally undetermined. Both certainly must be kept as near as possible together, for we desire no concentrations to the **detriment**[30] of personal unity, which is preserved by means of reflection. Their long and unbroken succession would create a tension, **incompatible**[31] with the existence of the healthy mind in the healthy body; in order then always to maintain the mind's **coherence**[32], instruction must follow the rule of giving equal weight in every smallest possible group of its objects reconcentration

>>> Unit 6 Steps in Instruction or Thinking

and reflection; that is to say, it must care equally and in regular succession for clearness of every particular, for association of the manifold, for coherent ordering of what is associated, and for a certain practice in progression through this order. Upon this depends the distinctness which must rule in all that is taught. The teacher's greatest difficulty here, perhaps, is to find real particulars—to analyse his own thoughts into their elements. Textbooks can in this case partly prepare the ground.

7. If however, instruction handles each little group of objects in this manner, many groups arise in the mind, and each one is grasped by a relative concentration until all are united in a higher reflection. But the union of the groups presupposes the perfect unity of each group. So long, therefore, as it is still possible for the last particular in the content of each group to fall apart from the rest, higher reflection cannot be thought of. But there is above this higher reflection a still higher, and so on indefinitely upwards, to the all-embracing highest, which we seek through the system of systems, but never reach. In earlier years nothing of this can be attempted; youth is always in an **intermediate**[33] state between concentration and distraction. We must be contented in earlier years with not attempting to give what we call system in the higher sense, but must on the other hand so much the more create clearness in every group; we must associate the groups the more **sedulously**[34] and variously, and be careful that the approach to the all-embracing reflection is made equally from all sides.

8. Upon this depends the **articulation**[35] of instruction. The larger members are composed of smaller, as are the lesser of the least. In each of the smallest members, four stages of instruction are to be distinguished; it must provide for Clearness, Association, Arrangement, and the Course of this order. These grades, which with the smallest members quickly succeed each other, follow one another more slowly, when those next in comprehensiveness are formed from the smallest members, and with ever-increasing spaces of time, as higher steps of reflection have to be climbed.

9. If we now look back on the analysis of the concept of interest, we find therein also, certain steps differentiated—Observation, Expectation, Demand and Action.

10. Observation depends on the relative power of a presentation to that of others which must yield to it—depends therefore partly on the intrinsic

strength of the one, partly on the ease with which the remainder yield. The latter leads to the idea of a discipline of thought, which we preferred to treat of specially in *The A B C of Anschauung*. The strength of a presentation can be partly attained through the power of the **sensuous**[36] impression (as, for example, through the simultaneous speaking of several children, also by the display of the same object in different ways with drawings, instruments, models, etc.), partly through the vividness of descriptions, especially if already connected presentations rest in the depths of the mind, which will unite with the one to be given. To effect this union generally, there is need of great skill and thought, which aims at anticipating future efforts by giving something to prepare the ground for them, as for instance *The A B C of Anschauung* does for mathematics, as the play of combinations does for grammar, and as narratives from **antiquity**[37] do for a classical author.

11. Through observation the singular becomes distinct, but association, order, and progress according to order, must also be observed.

12. In the same way we get clearness of the expectations and association of them, in fact, systematic and methodical expectation.

13. Nevertheless these complications do not now **claim**[38] our chief interest. We know that when the expected appears, only a new observation is produced. This is generally the case in the sphere of knowledge. Where some store of knowledge is already accumulated, it is not easy to observe anything to which expectations were not attached, yet the expectation dies out or becomes satisfied with new knowledge. If **vehement**[39] desires arise **therefrom**[40], they would fall under the rule of **temperance**[41] and consequently of discipline. But there is a species of observation which is not so easily satisfied or forgotten; there is a demand which is intended to be transformed into action; this is the demand for sympathy. Whatever rights then temperance exercises in this case, that education would nevertheless be a failure which did not leave behind resolutions to work for the good of humanity and society, as well as a certain energy of the religious **postulate**[42].

14. Accordingly, in the cultivation of sympathy, the higher steps to which interest may pass come much into consideration. And it is quite clear that these steps correspond with those of human life. In the child a sympathizing observation is appropriate, in the boy expectation, in the youth the demand for sympathy, that the man may act for it. The articulation of instruction,

>>> Unit 6 Steps in Instruction or Thinking

however, here permits again, even in the smallest subjects which belong to early years, demand (for sympathy) to be so **stimulated**[43] that it would pass into action. Out of such stimulations there grows in later years, assisted at the same time by the formation of character, that powerful demand which **begets**[44] actions.

15. Allow me briefly to define the results in few words, which can easily be understood.

Instruction must universally
- Point out,
- Connect,
- Teach,
- Philosophise.

16. In matters appertaining to sympathy it should be
- Observing,
- Continuous,
- Elevating,
- Active in the sphere of reality.

(From Johann Friedrich Herbart's "General Principles of the Science of Education Psychologically Deduced from Its Aim")

Vocabulary

1. **consecutively** /kənˈsekjətɪvli/
adv. happening one after the other without interruption 连续地;不间断地

2. **contemporaneously** /kənˌtempəˈreniəsli/
adv. happening or existing during the same period of time 同时发生(或存在)地;同时期地

3. **as it were**
to some extent 在某种程度上说
e.g. He is, as it were, a walking dictionary.

4. **dimension** /daɪˈmenʃn, dɪˈmenʃn/
n. a particular aspect 方面;部分
e.g. This adds a new dimension to our work.

5. **diverse** /daɪˈvɜːs/

adj. different 不同的；迥异的

e.g. Jones has a much more diverse and perhaps younger audience.

6. **succession** /səkˈseʃn/

n. a number of things that exist or happen one after the other 一连串；一系列；连续

e.g. Scoring three goals in quick succession, he made it 10－8.

7. **presuppose** /ˌpriːsəˈpəʊz/

v. take something else as the condition for something to be true or exist 预先假定；以……为前提；以……为先决条件

e.g. All your arguments presuppose that he's a rational, intelligent man.

8. **empirical** /ɪmˈpɪrɪkl/

adj. relying on practical experience rather than theories 经验主义的；以经验为依据的

e.g. There is no empirical evidence to support his thesis.

9. **betimes** /bɪˈtaɪmz/

adv. in good time 及时地

e.g. He awoke betimes that morning.

10. **thenceforward** /ˌðensˈfɔːwəd/

adv. from then on 从那时；其后

11. **expansion** /ɪkˈspænʃn/

n. the process of becoming greater in size, number, or amount 扩张；扩充

e.g. The rapid expansion of private health insurance shocked many people.

12. **manifold** /ˈmænɪfəʊld/

adj. of many different kinds 多样的；各种各样的

e.g. The difficulties are manifold.

13. **impediment** /ɪmˈpedɪmənt/

n. a person or thing that makes movement, development or progress difficult 妨碍；阻碍；障碍物

e.g. The level of inflation is a serious impediment to economic recovery.

14. **intervene** /ˌɪntəˈviːn/

v. become involved in something and try to change it 干涉；干预；介入

e.g. The situation calmed down when the police intervened.

15. **quota** /ˈkwəʊtə/

n. the limited number or quantity of something which is officially allowed 定量；定额

e.g. The quota of four tickets per person had been reduced to two.

16. **complication** /ˌkɒmplɪˈkeɪʃn/

n. a problem or difficulty that makes a situation harder to deal with 使情况复杂化的难题（或困难）

e. g. An added complication is the growing concern for the environment.

17. meditation /ˌmedɪˈteɪʃn/

n. the act of thinking about something very carefully and deeply for a long time 深思熟虑；苦思冥想

e. g. In his lonely meditations Antony had been forced to the conclusion that there had been rumours.

18. sphere /sfɪə/

n. area 范围

e. g. These countries are traditionally within the British or American spheres of influence.

19. subtle /ˈsʌtl/

adj. not immediately obvious or noticeable 不易察觉的；不明显的；微妙的

e. g. The slow and subtle changes have taken place in all living things.

20. feeble /ˈfiːbl/

adj. weak 虚弱的；微弱的；无力的

e. g. The feeble light of a tin lamp gave him some hope.

21. glimmer /ˈglɪmə/

v. produce or reflect a faint, gentle, often unsteady light 发微光；隐约闪烁

e. g. The glimmering ocean was so beautiful.

22. extinguish /ɪkˈstɪŋgwɪʃ/

v. destroy 消除；使破灭

e. g. The message extinguished her hopes of Richard's return.

23. kindle /ˈkɪndl/

v. make someone start to feel something 激起（感情）；使感受到

e. g. These poems have helped kindle the imagination of generations of children.

24. barbarous /ˈbɑːbərəs/

adj. rough and uncivilized 粗野的；未开化的；野蛮的

e. g. They used barbarous language.

25. divinity /dɪˈvɪnəti/

n. the quality of being divine 神性；神圣性

e. g. They have a lasting faith in the divinity of Christ's word.

26. presentiment /prɪˈzentɪmənt/

n. a feeling that a particular event, for example someone's death, will soon take place 预感；预知

e. g. He had a presentiment of disaster.

27. exercise /ˈeksəsaɪz/

v. use or put into effect 运用；行使

e. g. She has been reluctant to exercise her authority.

28. whence /wens/

adv. from what place or origin or source 从何处；来自何方

e. g. They returned whence they had come.

29. antitheses /ænˈtɪθəsiːz/

(pl of antithesis) a contrast between two things（二者间的）对比；对照

e. g. The antitheses between instinct and reason are obvious.

30. detriment /ˈdetrɪmənt/

n. harm or damage 伤害；损害

e. g. Children spend too much time on schoolwork, to the detriment of other activities.

31. incompatible /ˌɪnkəmˈpætəbl/

adj. very different in important ways 不能和谐相处的；不协调的；不一致的

e. g. His behavior has been incompatible with his role as head of state.

32. coherence /kəʊˈhɪərəns/

n. a state or situation in which all the parts or ideas fit together well so that they form a united whole 统一；一致性；连贯性

e. g. The anthology has a surprising sense of coherence.

33. intermediate /ˌɪntəˈmiːdiət/

adj. having some knowledge or skill but are not yet advanced 中等程度的；中级的

e. g. The Badminton Club holds coaching sessions for beginners and intermediate players on Friday evenings.

34. sedulously /ˈsedjʊləsli/

adv. in a sedulous manner 孜孜不倦地；刻意地

35. articulation /ɑːˌtɪkjuˈleɪʃn/

n. the expression of ideas, especially in words（思想或感情的）表达

e. g. This was seen as a way of restricting women's articulation of grievances.

36. sensuous /ˈsenʃuəs/

adj. giving pleasure to the mind or body through the senses 愉悦感官的；给人以美感的

e. g. It is a sensuous but demanding car to drive.

37. antiquity /ænˈtɪkwəti/

n. the distant past, especially the time of the ancient Egyptians, Greeks, and Romans 古代；古时（尤指古埃及、古希腊、古罗马时期）

e. g. We were impressed by the famous monuments of classical antiquity.

38. claim /kleɪm/

v. gain or win 取得；获得；赢得

e. g. Steffi Graf claimed a fourth Wimbledon title in 1992.

>>> Unit 6 Steps in Instruction or Thinking

39. vehement /ˈviːəmənt/

adj. having very strong feelings or opinions and expressing them forcefully 激情的；激烈的

e. g. The proposal has faced vehement opposition from many teachers.

40. therefrom /ˌðeəˈfrɒm/

adv. from that circumstance or source; from that place or from there 由此；从那里

e. g. The committee will examine the agreement and any problems arising therefrom.

41. temperance /ˈtempərəns/

n. possession of a strong mind so as not to eat too much, drink too much, or do too much of anything 节制；有分寸；自我克制

e. g. His lifestyle was marked by temperance.

42. postulate /ˈpɒstjuleɪt/

v. suggest something as the basis for a theory, argument, or calculation, or assume that it is the basis 假定；假设

e. g. Scientists have postulated the existence of water on the planet.

43. stimulate /ˈstɪmjuleɪt/

v. encourage something to begin or develop further 刺激；激励；促使

e. g. A raise in employee wages might stimulate production.

44. beget /bɪˈget/

v. cause something to happen or be created 招致；导致；引起

e. g. Violence begets more violence.

Exercises for Text 1

I. Read the text and answer the questions.

1. What are the two things that instruction should develop at the same time?
2. What should adults be like if they want to understand children?
3. What are the four steps in the education of knowledge?
4. What are the four steps of interest?
5. What are the implications of Herbart's four steps in modern education?

II. Complete the sentences with the words below. Change the form where necessary.

presentiment	exercise	kindle	incompatible	sensuous
meditation	as it were	sphere	glimmer	postulate
claim	complication	presuppose	subtle	stimulate
intervene	succession	manifold	feeble	vehement

1. I'd understood the words, but I didn't, _____, understand the question.
2. Now they are returning to _____ what was theirs.
3. Adams took a(n) _____ of jobs which have stood him in good stead.
4. The end of an era _____ the start of another.
5. The language can be learnt here in _____ forms. You can choose the one you like.
6. The company is doing nothing to _____ in the crisis.
7. The age difference was a(n) _____ to the relationship. It will make the relationship more complicated.
8. The man, lost in _____, walked with slow steps along the shore.
9. They see the region as their natural _____ of influence due to their historical links and a shared language.
10. Intolerance can take _____ forms too and those forms can hurt people more.
11. He told them he was old and _____ and was not able to walk so far.
12. The moon _____ faintly through the mists.
13. The second world war _____ his enthusiasm for politics.
14. I had a(n) _____ that he represented a danger to me.
15. They are merely _____ their right to holidays.
16. They feel strongly that their religion is _____ with the philosophy.
17. The film is ravishing to look at and boasts a(n) _____ musical score.
18. She suddenly became very _____ and agitated, jumping around and shouting.
19. Freud _____ that we all have a death instinct as well as a life instinct.
20. The city health service has _____ public interest in home cures.

III. Translate the sentences into Chinese.

1. For a beginning is always made at the same time from several sides, and much always must be prepared by what had gone before.
2. Our preceding concepts show us that instruction has to develop knowledge and sympathy at the same time, as diverse and fundamentally individual states of mind.
3. And how much more rapidly would it develop were we to present to it at first the simplest relationships, and not throw it at once into incomprehensible complications.
4. It is a matter of course that teachers to perceive what is moving in the children's minds must themselves possess that same culture, the most subtle traces of which they have to observe in them.
5. The varieties of interest then which instruction ought to cultivate, present to us only differences in things simultaneously, but not a distinct succession of steps.

>>> Unit 6 Steps in Instruction or Thinking

READING
& CRITICAL
THINKING

Text 2

The Five Logical Steps

John Dewey

1. Upon examination, each instance reveals, more or less clearly, five logically distinct steps: (i) a felt difficulty; (ii) its location and definition; (iii) suggestion of possible solution; (iv) development by reasoning of the bearings of the suggestion; (v) further observation and experiment leading to its acceptance or rejection; that is, the conclusion of belief or disbelief.

2. The first and second steps frequently **fuse**[1] into one. The difficulty may be felt with sufficient definiteness as to set the mind at once speculating upon its probable solution, or an undefined uneasiness and shock may come first, leading only later to definite attempt to find out what is the matter. Whether the two steps are distinct or blended, there is the factor emphasized in our original account of reflection—viz. the **perplexity**[2] or problem. In the first of the three cases cited, the difficulty **resides**[3] in the conflict between conditions at hand and a desired and intended result, between an end and the means for reaching it. The purpose of keeping an engagement at a certain time, and the existing hour taken in connection with the location, are not **congruous**[4]. The object of thinking is to introduce **congruity**[5] between the two. The given conditions themselves cannot be altered; time will not go backward nor will the distance between the 16th Street and the 124th Street shorten itself. The problem is the discovery of intervening terms which when inserted between the remoter end and the given means will harmonise them with each other.

3. In the second case, the difficulty experienced is the **incompatibility**[6] of a suggested and (temporarily) accepted belief that the pole is a flagpole, with certain other facts. Suppose we symbolize the qualities that suggest *flagpole* by the letter a, b, c; those that oppose this suggestion as p, q, r. There is, of course, nothing inconsistent in the qualities themselves; but in pulling the mind to different and incongruous conclusions they conflict—hence the problem ...

4. In the third case, an observer trained to the idea of natural laws or uniformities finds something odd or exceptional in the behavior of the bubbles. The problem is to reduce the apparent **anomalies**[7] to instances of well-established laws. Here the method of solution is also to seek for intermediary terms which will connect, by regular linkage, the seemingly extraordinary movements of the bubbles with the conditions known to follow from processes supposed to be operative.

5. As already noted, the first two steps, the feeling of a **discrepancy**[8], or difficulty, and the acts of observation that serve to define the character of the difficulty may, in a given instance, **telescope**[9] together. In cases of striking **novelty**[10] or unusual perplexity, the difficulty, however, is likely to present itself at first as a shock, as emotional disturbance, as a more or less vague feeling of the unexpected, of something queer, strange, funny, or **disconcerting**[11]. In such instances, there are necessary observations deliberately calculated to **bring to light**[12] just what is the trouble, or to make clear the specific character of the problem. In large measure, the existence or non-existence of this step makes the difference between reflection **proper**[13], or safeguarded critical **inference**[14] and uncontrolled thinking. Where sufficient pains to locate the difficulty are not taken, suggestions for its resolution must be more or less random. Imagine a doctor called in to prescribe for a patient. The patient tells him some things that are wrong; his experienced eye, at a glance, takes in other signs of a certain disease. But if he permits the suggestion of this special disease to take possession **prematurely**[15] of his mind, to become an accepted conclusion, his scientific thinking is by that much cut short. A large part of his technique, as a skilled practitioner, is to prevent the acceptance of the first suggestions that arise; even, indeed, to postpone the occurrence of any very definite suggestion till the trouble—the nature of the problem—has been thoroughly explored. In the case of a physician this proceeding is known as diagnosis, but a similar inspection is required in every **novel**[16] and complicated situation to prevent rushing to a conclusion. The essence of critical thinking is suspended judgment; and the essence of this suspense is inquiry to determine the nature of the problem before proceeding to attempts at its solution. This, more than any other thing, transforms mere inference into tested inference, suggested conclusions into proof.

>>> Unit 6 Steps in Instruction or Thinking

6. The third factor is suggestion. The situation in which the perplexity occurs calls up something not present to the senses: the present location, the thought of subway or elevated train; the stick before the eyes, the idea of a flagpole, an ornament, an apparatus for wireless telegraphy; the soap bubbles, the law of expansion of bodies through heat and of their contraction through cold. (a) Suggestion is the very heart of inference; it involves going from what is present to something absent. Hence, it is more or less speculative, adventurous. Since inference goes beyond what is actually present, it involves a leap, a jump, the propriety of which cannot be absolutely **warranted**[17] in advance, no matter what precautions be taken. Its control is indirect, on the one hand, involving the formation of habits of mind which are at once **enterprising**[18] and cautious; and on the other hand, involving the selection and arrangement of the particular facts upon perception of which suggestion issues. (b) The suggested conclusion so far as it is not accepted but only tentatively entertained constitutes an idea. Synonyms for this are supposition, **conjecture**[19], guess, **hypothesis**[20], and (in elaborate cases) theory. Since suspended belief, or the postponement of a final conclusion **pending**[21] further evidence, depends partly upon the presence of rival conjectures as to the best course to pursue or the probable explanation to favor, cultivation of a variety of alternative suggestions is an important factor in good thinking.

7. The process of developing the bearings—or, as they are more technically termed, the implications—of any idea with respect to any problem, is termed reasoning. As an idea is inferred from given facts, so reasoning sets out from an idea. The idea of elevated road is developed into the idea of difficulty of locating station, length of time occupied on the journey, distance of station at the other end from place to be reached. In the second case, the implication of a flagpole is seen to be a vertical position; of a wireless apparatus, location on a high part of the ship and, moreover, absence from every casual tugboat; while the idea of index to direction in which the boat moves, when developed, is found to cover all the details of the case.

8. Reasoning has the same effect upon a suggested solution as more intimate and **extensive**[22] observation has upon the original problem. Acceptance of the suggestion in its first form is prevented by looking into it more thoroughly. Conjectures that seem **plausible**[23] at first sight are often

found unfit or even absurd when their full consequences are traced out. Even when reasoning out the bearings of a supposition does not lead to rejection, it develops the idea into a form in which it is more **apposite**[24] to the problem. Only when, for example, the conjecture that a pole was an index-pole had been thought out into its bearings could its particular applicability to the case in hand be judged. Suggestions at first seemingly remote and wild are frequently so transformed by being elaborated into what follows from them as to become apt and fruitful. The development of an idea through reasoning helps at least to supply the intervening or intermediate terms that link together into a consistent whole apparently **discrepant**[25] extremes.

9. The concluding and conclusive step is some kind of experimental **corroboration**[26], or **verification**[27], of the conjectural idea. Reasoning shows that if the idea be adopted, certain consequences follow. So far, the conclusion is hypothetical or conditional. If we look and find present all the conditions demanded by the theory, and if we find the characteristic traits called for by rival alternatives to be lacking, the tendency to believe, to accept, is almost irresistible. Sometimes direct observation **furnishes**[28] corroboration, as in the case of the pole on the boat. In other cases, as in that of the bubbles, experiment is required; that is, conditions are deliberately arranged in accord with the requirements of an idea or hypothesis to see if the results theoretically indicated by the idea actually occur. If it is found that the experimental results agree with the theoretical, or rationally deduced, results, and if there is reason to believe that only the conditions in question would yield such results, the confirmation is so strong as to induce a conclusion—at least until **contrary**[29] facts shall indicate the **advisability**[30] of its **revision**[31].

10. Observation exists at the beginning and again at the end of the process: at the beginning, to determine more definitely and precisely the nature of the difficulty to be dealt with; at the end, to test the value of some hypothetically entertained conclusion. Between those two **termini**[32] of observation, we find the more distinctively mental aspects of the entire thought-cycle: (i) inference, the suggestion of an explanation or solution; and (ii) reasoning, the development of the bearings and implications of the suggestion. Reasoning requires some experimental observation to confirm it, while experiment can be economically and fruitfully conducted only on the basis of an idea that has been tentatively developed by reasoning.

>>> Unit 6　Steps in Instruction or Thinking

11. The disciplined, or logically trained, mind—the aim of the educative process—is the mind able to judge how far each of these steps needs to be carried in any particular situation. No **cast-iron**[33] rules can be laid down. Each case has to be dealt with as it arises, on the basis of its importance and of the context in which it occurs. To take too much pains in one case is as foolish—as illogical—as to take too little in another. At one extreme, almost any conclusion that insures prompt and unified action may be better than any long-delayed conclusion; while at the other, decision may have to be postponed for a long period—perhaps for a life-time. The trained mind is the one that best grasps the degree of observation, forming of ideas, reasoning, and experimental testing required in any special case, and that profits the most, in future thinking, by mistakes made in the past. What is important is that the mind should be sensitive to problems and skilled in methods of attack and solution.

(From John Dewey's *How We Think*)

Vocabulary

1. **fuse** /fjuːz/
v. mix together different elements 融化；融合
e. g. During the reaction the atoms fuse together.

2. **perplexity** /pəˈpleksəti/
n. trouble or confusion resulting from complexity 困惑；混乱；复杂；困难
e. g. He began counting them and then, with growing perplexity, counted them a second time.

3. **reside** /rɪˈzaɪd/
v. make one's home or live in 居住；属于；存在
e. g. He spent most of his time in Rutherglen, where his family resided.

4. **congruous** /ˈkɒngruəs/
adj. suitable or appropriate together 一致的
e. g. The work is congruous to his character.

5. **congruity** /kənˈgruːɪti/
n. the state of being suitable or appropriate together 一致

6. incompatibility /ˌɪnkəmˌpætəˈbɪləti/

n. the relation between propositions that cannot both be true at the same time 不相容；不和谐

7. anomaly /əˈnɒməli/

n. deviation from the normal or common order or form or rule 异常；反常

e. g. A storm like that is an anomaly for this area.

8. discrepancy /dɪsˈkrepənsi/

n. a difference between conflicting facts or claims or opinions 差异；不一致

e. g. As stipulated in the contract, a minor discrepancy in colors is permissible.

9. telescope /ˈtelɪskəʊp/

v. crush together or collapse 叠缩

e. g. The fishing rod telescopes into its handle.

10. novelty /ˈnɒvlti/

n. originality by virtue of being new and surprising 新奇

e. g. The toy's novelty soon wore off.

11. disconcerting /ˌdɪskənˈsɜːtɪŋ/

adj. causing an emotional disturbance 令人困惑的；令人不安的

e. g. The stories I had heard were coming back in disconcerting detail.

12. bring to light

make ... known 揭露；暴露

e. g. I will bring to light the truth so that fewer people will be cheated.

13. proper /ˈprɒpə/

adj. limited to the thing specified 本身的；正式的

e. g. The city centre proper was destroyed by the fire.

14. inference /ˈɪnfərəns/

n. the reasoning involved in drawing a conclusion or making a logical judgment on the basis of circumstantial evidence and prior conclusions rather than on the basis of direct observation 推理

e. g. Its existence is only known by inference.

15. prematurely /ˌprɪməˈtʃə(r)li/

adv. too soon; in a premature manner 过早地；贸然地

e. g. The law could arrest the development of good research if applied prematurely.

16. novel /ˈnɒvl/

adj. of a kind not seen before 新颖的

e. g. She has suggested a novel approach to the problem.

17. warrant /ˈwɒrənt/

v. show to be reasonable or provide adequate ground for 使有必要（或正当）

e. g. This report warrants careful study.

>>> Unit 6   Steps in Instruction or Thinking

18. **enterprising** /ˈentəpraɪzɪŋ/

adj. marked by aggressive ambition, energy and initiative 有进取心的；有创业精神的

e. g. As an enterprising young reporter, she covered many important stories.

19. **conjecture** /kənˈdʒektʃə/

n. reasoning that involves the formation of conclusions from incomplete evidence 推测；猜想

e. g. There has been some conjecture about a possible merger.

20. **hypothesis** /haɪˈpɒθəsɪs/

n. a tentative theory about the natural world; a concept that is not yet verified but that if true would explain certain facts or phenomena 假设；假说

e. g. Their hypothesis is that watching excessive amounts of television reduces a person's ability to concentrate.

21. **pending** /ˈpendɪŋ/

prep. awaiting conclusion or confirmation 直到

e. g. He is being held in jail pending trial.

22. **extensive** /ɪkˈstensɪv/

adj. having broad range or effect 范围广泛的

e. g. The storm caused extensive damage.

23. **plausible** /ˈplɔːzəbl/

adj. apparently reasonable and valid 貌似真实的；貌似有理的

e. g. The only plausible explanation is that he forgot.

24. **apposite** /ˈæpəzɪt/

adj. being of striking appropriateness and pertinence 恰当的；适当的

e. g. The poem was an apposite choice for the ceremony.

25. **discrepant** /dɪˈskrepənt/

adj. not compatible with other facts 差异的

26. **corroboration** /kəˌrɒbəˈreɪʃn/

n. confirmation that some fact or statement is true 进一步的证实

e. g. The witness was unable to provide corroboration of what he had told the police.

27. **verification** /ˌverɪfɪˈkeɪʃn/

n. additional proof that something that was believed (some fact or hypothesis or theory) is correct 进一步的证实

e. g. The credit card is then accepted, subject to verification of the signature.

28. **furnish** /ˈfɜːnɪʃ/

v. provide or furnish with 提供

e. g. Will these findings furnish more information on prehistoric man?

113

29. **contrary** /ˈkɒntrəri/

adj. very opposed in nature or character or purpose 相反的

e. g. In the end the contrary was proved true: he was innocent and she was guilty.

30. **advisability** /ədˌvaɪzəˈbɪləti/

n. the quality of being advisable 明智；合理性

e. g. I have doubts about the advisability of surgery in this case.

31. **revision** /rɪˈvɪʒn/

n. the act of revising or altering (involving reconsideration and modification) 修订

e. g. A revision of the theory will be necessary.

32. **termini** /ˈtɜːmmaɪ/

n. plural form of terminus 目的地；终点

33. **cast-iron** /ˌkɑːstˈaɪən/

adj. extremely robust 严格的

e. g. It's a cast-iron excuse that most people will believe.

Exercises for Text 2

I. Decide whether the statements are true (T) or false (F) according to the text.

1. The essence of critical thinking is not to judge hastily but to determine the nature of the problem before trying to solve it.
2. Although inference goes beyond what is present, it can be warranted in advance so long as we take enough precautions.
3. Conjectures that seem reasonable at first are always found to be reasonable when their consequences are known.
4. If the characteristic traits of rival alternatives of a theory are lacking, then we have reasons to believe the theory.
5. Sometimes we need direct observation to believe a theory; sometimes we need an experiment to test a theory.

II. Translate the following sentences with the key words in the parentheses.

1. 年轻人在生活中会面临很多困惑。(perplexity)
2. 他在国外居住多年以后，于1939年回到了英国。(reside)
3. 他的行动和他信奉的原则一致。(compatible)
4. 女生和男生在学校表现不同,原因是什么呢？(discrepancy)
5. 接待处不临街,这多少让人有点想不通。(disconcerting)
6. 这场研讨会目的是还原事情的真相,消除一般人的误解。(bring ... to light)
7. 正式面试之前的友好闲聊是为了放松候选人的心情。(proper)

8. 我得到的结果证明这个猜想事实上是正确的。(conjecture)

9. 他的叙述听上去很合理,所以我们都相信了。(plausible)

10. 她向他提供了与案件有关的事实。(furnish)

III. Explain the following sentences in your own words.

1. Suggestions at first seemingly remote and wild are frequently so transformed by being elaborated into what follows from them as to become apt and fruitful.

2. Conditions are deliberately arranged in accord with the requirements of an idea or hypothesis to see if the results theoretically indicated by the idea actually occur.

3. The disciplined, or logically trained, mind—the aim of the educative process—is the mind able to judge how far each of these steps needs to be carried in any particular situation.

4. Each case has to be dealt with as it arises, on the basis of its importance and of the context in which it occurs.

5. What is important is that the mind should be sensitive to problems and skilled in methods of attack and solution.

Learning Strategies

Reading classic writing can improve your language and help you better understand the writer's ideas. But this will not happen by magic: only if you read the article carefully and think about what you are reading. First, if you concentrate hard, you will not only enlarge your vocabulary, but also begin to distinguish slight differences in meaning between words. Secondly, if you examine the language carefully, you can learn to appreciate different English writing styles.

It is necessary to read an article more than once in order to absorb its full benefit. For example, we can read the first article once to understand that the article is about instruction, once again to understand that the main idea is the four steps of instruction and finally understand the ideas of Herbart on education.

We suggest that you read each article for at least three times, with each time for different purposes.

Unit Project

Work in groups to make research on articles about the steps of teaching or thinking and make a pamphlet about it.

1. Find articles related to steps in English teaching or thinking and sum up their views.
2. Hold a discussion in groups about whether you agree with the views of those articles.
3. Give an analysis of those articles by using the two authors' views.
4. Make a pamphlet about it.

>>> Unit 7 Why Should Science Be Taught in Schools?

Unit 7

Why Should Science Be Taught in Schools?

Pre-reading questions:

1. What do you know about Spenser's view on the aim of education?
2. What do you think is the relationship between science and arts?

READING & CRITICAL THINKING

Text 1

What Knowledge Is of Most Worth?

Herbert Spencer

1. In education, then, this is the question of Questions, which it is high time we discussed in some **methodic**¹ way. The first in importance, though the last to be considered, is the problem—how to decide among the conflicting claims of various subjects on our attention. Before there can be a **rational**² curriculum, we must settle which things it most concerns us to know; or, to use a word of Bacon's, now unfortunately **obsolete**³—we must determine the relative values of knowledges.

2. To this end, a measure of value is the first **requisite**⁴. And happily, respecting the true measure of value, as expressed in general terms, there can be no dispute. Everyone in contending for the worth of any particular order of information, does so by showing its bearing upon some part of life. In reply to the question "Of what use is it?", the mathematician, linguist, naturalist, or philosopher explains the way in which his learning beneficially influences action—saves from evil or secures good—**conduces**⁵ to happiness. When the teacher of writing has pointed out how great an aid writing is to success in business—that is, to the obtainment of sustenance—that is, to satisfactory living; he is held to have proved his case. And when the collector of dead facts (say a numismatist) fails to make clear any appreciable effects which these facts can produce on human welfare, he is obliged to admit that they are comparatively valueless. All then, either directly or by implication, appeal to this as the ultimate test.

3. How to live?—that is the essential question for us. Not how to live in the mere material sense only, but in the widest sense. The general problem which **comprehends**⁶ every special problem is—the right ruling of conduct in all directions under all circumstances. In what way to treat the body; in what way to the mind; in what way to manage our affairs; in what way to bring

up a family; in what way to behave as a citizen; in what way to **utilize**[7] those sources of happiness which nature supplies—how to use all our **faculties**[8] to the greatest advantage of ourselves. Thing needful for us to learn, is, by consequence, the great thing which education has to teach. To prepare us for complete living is the function which education has to **discharge**[9]; and the only rational mode of judging of an educational course is to judge in what degree it discharges such function …

4. Our first step must obviously be to **classify**[10], in the order of their importance, the leading kinds of activity which constitute human life. They may be naturally arranged into: a) those activities which directly **minister to**[11] self-**preservation**[12]; b) those activities which, by securing the necessaries of life, indirectly minister to self-preservation; c) those activities which have for their end the rearing and discipline of offspring; d) those activities which are involved in the maintenance of proper social and political relations; e) those **miscellaneous**[13] activities which fill up the leisure part of life, devoted to the **gratification**[14] of the tastes and feelings.

5. That these stand in something like their true order of subordination, it needs no long consideration to show. The actions and **precautions**[15] by which, from moment to moment, we secure personal safety, must clearly take precedence of all others. Could there be a man, ignorant as an infant of all surrounding objects and movements, or how to guide himself among them, he would pretty certainly lose his life the first time he went into the street: **notwithstanding**[16] any amount of learning he might have on other matters. And as entire ignorance in all other directions would be less promptly fatal than entire ignorance in this direction, it must be admitted that knowledge immediately **conducive**[17] to self-preservation is of primary importance.

6. That next after direct self-preservation comes the indirect self-preservation which consists in acquiring the means of living, none will question. That a man's industrial functions must be considered before his parental ones, is manifest from the fact that, speaking generally, the discharge of the parental functions is made possible only by the previous discharge of the industrial ones. The power of self-maintenance necessarily preceding the power of maintaining offspring, it follows that knowledge needful for self-maintenance has stronger claims than knowledge needful for family welfare—is second in value to none **save**[18] knowledge needful for immediate self-preservation.

7. As the family comes before the State in order of time—as the bringing up of children is possible before the State exists, or when it has ceased to be, whereas the State is rendered possible only by the bringing up of children; it follows that the duties of the parent demand closer attention than those of the citizen. Or, to use a further argument—since the goodness of a society ultimately depends on the nature of its citizens; and since the nature of its citizens is more **modifiable**[19] by early training than by anything else; we must conclude that the welfare of the family **underlies**[20] the welfare of society. And hence knowledge directly conducing to the first must take **precedence**[21] of knowledge directly conducing to the last.

8. Those various forms of pleasurable occupation which fill up the leisure left by graver occupations—the enjoyments of music, poetry, painting, etc.—manifestly imply a preexisting society. Not only is a considerable development of them impossible without a long-established social union, but their very subject-matter consists in great part of social **sentiments**[22] and sympathies. Not only does society supply the conditions to their growth, but also the ideas and sentiments they express. And, consequently, that part of human conduct which constitutes good citizenship is of more moment than that which goes out in accomplishments or exercise of the tastes; and, in education, preparation for the one must rank before preparation for the other.

9. Such then, we repeat, is something like the rational order of subordination: That education which prepares for direct self-preservation, that which prepares for indirect self-preservation, that which prepares for parenthood, that which prepares for citizenship, that which prepares for the miscellaneous refinements of life …

10. We conclude, then, that for discipline, as well as for guidance, science is of chiefest value. In all its effects, learning the meaning of things is better than learning the meanings of words. Whether for intellectual, moral, or religious training, the study of surrounding phenomena is immensely superior to the study of grammars and lexicons.

11. Thus to the question we set out with—What knowledge is of most worth?—the uniform reply is Science. For direct self-important knowledge is Science. For that indirect self-preservation which we call gaining a livelihood, the knowledge of greatest value is Science. For the due discharge of parental functions, the proper guidance is to be found only in Science. For that

interpretation of national life, past and present, without which the citizen cannot rightly regulate his conduct, the **indispensable**[23] key is Science. Alike for the most perfect production and highest enjoyment of arts in all its forms, the needful preparation is still Science.

(From Herbert Spencer's *What Knowledge Is of Most Worth?*)

Vocabulary

1. **methodic** /mɪˈθɒdɪk/

adj. in an organized way 有条理的;有组织的

2. **rational** /ˈræʃnəl/

adj. based on reason rather than on emotion 理性的;合理的

e.g. He's asking you to look at both sides of the case and come to a rational decision.

3. **obsolete** /ˈɒbsəliːt/

adj. no longer needed because something better has been invented 过时的;废弃的;淘汰的

e.g. So much equipment becomes obsolete almost as soon as it's made.

4. **requisite** /ˈrekwɪzɪt/

n. something which is necessary for a particular purpose 必需品;必备品;必要条件

e.g. An understanding of accounting techniques is a major requisite for the work of the analysts.

5. **conduce** /kənˈdjuːs/

v. benefit 有益于;对……有贡献

e.g. Wealth does not always conduce to happiness.

6. **comprehend** /ˌkɒmprɪˈhend/

v. include 包含

e.g. Science comprehends many disciplines.

7. **utilize** /ˈjuːtəlaɪz/

v. use 利用;使用

e.g. Sound engineers utilize a range of techniques to enhance the quality of the recordings.

8. faculty /ˈfæklti/

n. physical and mental abilities 官能；能力

e. g. He was drunk and not in control of his faculties.

9. discharge /dɪsˈtʃɑːdʒ, ˈdɪstʃɑːdʒ/

v. do everything that needs to be done 履行（职责）；完成（任务）

e. g. The city must discharge its legal duty to house the homeless.

10. classify /ˈklæsɪfaɪ/

v. divide things into groups or types so that things with similar characteristics are in the same group 把……分类；为……归类

e. g. It is necessary initially to classify the headaches into certain types, so that it will make doctors' work easier.

11. minister to

help; give 帮助

12. preservation /ˌprezəˈveɪʃn/

n. the act of taking action to save something or protect it from damage or decay 保持

13. miscellaneous /ˌmɪsəˈleɪniəs/

adj. consisting of many different kinds of things or people that are difficult to put into a particular category 混杂的；五花八门的；各式各样的

e. g. They eat a lot of meats and dairy foods, along with a lot of miscellaneous items that don't fall into any group.

14. gratification /ˌɡrætɪfɪˈkeɪʃn/

n. satisfaction; joy 满意；满足；喜悦

e. g. A feed will usually provide instant gratification to a crying baby.

15. precaution /prɪˈkɔːʃn/

n. an action that is intended to prevent something dangerous or unpleasant from happening 预防措施；防备

e. g. Could he not, just as a precaution, move to a place of safety?

16. notwithstanding /ˌnɒtwɪθˈstændɪŋ/

prep. in spite of 尽管

e. g. He despised William Pitt, notwithstanding the similar views they both held.

17. conducive /kənˈdjuːsɪv/

adj. making the other thing likely to happen 有助的；有益的

e. g. Make your bedroom as conducive to sleep as possible.

18. save /seɪv/

prep. except 除……之外

e. g. There is almost no water at all in Mochudi save that brought up from bore holes.

19. modifiable /ˈmɒdɪfaɪəbl/

adj. capable of being modified in form, character or strength (especially by making less extreme) 可更改的

20. underlie /ˌʌndəˈlaɪ/

v. be the cause or basis of something 为……的起因；构成……的基础

e. g. Try to figure out what feeling underlies your anger.

21. precedence /ˈpresɪdəns/

n. the condition of being more important than somebody else and therefore coming or being dealt with first 优先；优先权

e. g. Have as much fun as possible at college, but don't let it take precedence over work.

22. sentiment /ˈsentɪmənt/

n. an idea or feeling that someone expresses in words（用言辞表达的）见解；感想

e. g. The Foreign Secretary echoed this sentiment.

23. indispensable /ˌɪndɪˈspensəbl/

adj. absolutely essential 必不可少的；不可或缺的

e. g. A calculator is an indispensable tool for solving these problems.

Exercises for Text 1

I. Read the text and answer the questions.

1. What is the most important issue in education?
2. What is the purpose of education?
3. Why are the subjects related to self-preservation the most important ones?
4. What are the least important subjects? Why?
5. Why is science the most important subject in school?

II. Complete the sentences with the words below. Change the form where necessary.

faculty	sentiment	comprehend	precedence	requisite
precaution	conduce	classify	indispensable	utilize
miscellaneous	notwithstanding	conducive	underlie	gratification
rational	minister to	obsolete	constitute	discharge

1. I must agree with the _____ expressed by John Prescott.
2. It is also a myth that the _____ of hearing is greatly increased in blind people.
3. I had taken the _____ of doing a little research before I made the decision.
4. Rocks can be _____ according to their mode of origin.
5. The possession of wealth does not always _____ to happiness.

6. As the King's representative, he was so important that he took _____ over everyone else on the island.
7. _____ differences, there are clear similarities in all of the world's religions.
8. A good dictionary is _____ for learning a foreign language.
9. A university degree has become a(n) _____ for entry into most professions.
10. Sometimes the noisy home environment just isn't _____ to reading.
11. Asia _____ many nations and there is lots of cooperation between those nations.
12. They receive a grant of ￡1,094 to cover the cost of _____ expenses.
13. When we are angry, we need to calm down and figure out what feelings _____ our anger.
14. Self-discipline and the ability to delay _____ are very important factors for success.
15. We must consider how best to _____ what resources we have.
16. Volunteers _____ more than 95% of the Center's work force.
17. As a leader, he needs to _____ his role and gather people together to do something meaningful.
18. So many instruments have become _____ almost as soon as they are made. It's really a great waste.
19. We need to look at both sides of the case before we can come to a(n) _____ decision.
20. She felt it was her vocation to _____ the sick, so she went out of her way to take care of the sick child for the whole night.

III. Translate the sentences into Chinese.

1. Everyone in contending for the worth of any particular order of information does so by showing its bearing upon some part of life.
2. That these stand in something like their true order of subordination, it needs no long consideration to show.
3. The general problem which comprehends every special problem is—the right ruling of conduct in all directions under all circumstances.
4. Whether for intellectual, moral, or religious training, the study of surrounding phenomena is immensely superior to the study of grammars and lexicons.
5. Alike for the most perfect production and highest enjoyment of arts in all its forms, the needful preparation is still Science.

>>> Unit 7 Why Should Science Be Taught in Schools?

READING
& CRITICAL
THINKING

Text 2

Science and Education

Thomas Henry Huxley

1. So far as school education is concerned, I want to go no further just now; and I believe that such instruction would make an excellent introduction to that **preparatory**[1] scientific training which, as I have indicated, is so essential for the successful pursuit of our most important professions. But this **modicum**[2] of instruction must be so given as to ensure real knowledge and practical discipline. If scientific education is to be dealt with as mere bookwork, it will be better not to attempt it, but to stick to the Latin Grammar which makes no pretense to be anything but bookwork.

2. If the great benefits of scientific training are sought, it is essential that such training should be real: that is to say, that the mind of the scholar should be brought into direct relation with fact, that he should not merely be told a thing, but made to see by the use of his own intellect and ability that the thing is so and no otherwise. The great **peculiarity**[3] of scientific training, that in virtue of which it cannot be replaced by any other discipline whatsoever, is this bringing of the mind directly into contact with fact, and practicing the intellect in the completest form of **induction**[4]; that is to say, in drawing conclusions from particular facts made known by immediate observation of Nature.

3. The other studies which enter into ordinary education do not discipline the mind in this way. Mathematical training is almost purely **deductive**[5]. The mathematician starts with a few simple propositions, the proof of which is so obvious that they are called **self-evident**[6], and the rest of his work consists of subtle **deductions**[7] from them. The teaching of languages, at any rate as ordinarily practised, is of the same general nature—authority and tradition furnish the data, and the mental operations of the scholar are deductive.

4. Again if history be the subject of study, the facts are still taken upon the evidence of tradition and authority. You cannot make a boy see the battle of Thermopylae for himself or know, of his own knowledge, that Cromwell once ruled England. There is no getting into direct contact with natural fact by this road; there is no **dispensing with**[8] authority, but rather a resting upon it.

5. In all these respects, science differs from other educational discipline, and prepares the scholars for common life. What have we to do in everyday life? Most of the business which demands our attentions is matter of act, which needs, in the first place, to be accurately observed or **apprehended**[9]; in the second, to be interpreted by **inductive**[10] and deductive reasonings, which are altogether similar in their nature to those employed in science. In the one case, as in the other, whatever is taken for granted is so taken **at one's own peril**[11]; fact and reason are the ultimate **arbiters**[12], and patience and honesty are the great helpers out of difficulty.

6. But if scientific training is to yield its most **eminent**[13] results, it must, I repeat, be made practical. That is to say, in explaining to a child the general phenomena of Nature, you must, as far as possible, give reality to your teaching by object-lessons; in teaching him botany, he must handle the plants and **dissect**[14] the flowers for himself; in teaching him physics and chemistry, you must not be **solicitous**[15] to fill him with information, but you must be careful that what he learns he knows of his own knowledge. Don't be satisfied with telling him that a magnet attracts iron. Let him see that it does; let him feel the pull of the one upon the other for himself. And, especially, tell him that it is his duty to doubt until he is **compelled**[16], by the absolute authority of Nature, to believe that which is written in books. Pursue this discipline carefully and **conscientiously**[17], and you may make sure that, however **scanty**[18] may be the measure of information which you have poured into the boy's mind, you have created an intellectual habit of priceless value in practical life.

7. One is constantly asked, when should this scientific education be **commenced**[19]? I should say with the dawn of intelligence. As I have already said, a child seeks for information about matters of physical science as soon as it begins to talk. The first teaching it wants is an object-lesson of one sort or another; and as soon as it is fit for systematic instruction of any kind, it is fit for a modicum of science.

8. People talk of the difficulty of teaching young children such matters, and in the same breath insist upon their learning their **Catechism**[20], which contains propositions far harder to **comprehend**[21] than anything in the educational course I have proposed. Again I am **incessantly**[22] told that we, who advocate the introduction of science in schools, make no allowance for the stupidity of the average boy or girl; but in my belief that **stupidity**[23], in nine cases out of ten, is developed by a long process of parental and **pedagogic**[24] **repression**[25] of the natural intellectual appetites, accompanied by a persistent attempt to create artificial ones for food which is not only tasteless, but essentially **indigestible**[26].

9. Those who urge the difficulty of instructing young people in science are apt to forget another very important condition of success—important in all kinds of teaching, but most essential, I am **disposed**[27] to think, when the scholars are very young. This condition is that the teacher should himself really and practically know his subject. If he does, he will be able to speak of it in the easy language, and with the completeness of **conviction**[28], with which he talks of any ordinary everyday matter. If he does not, he will be afraid to wander beyond the limits of the technical **phraseology**[29] which he has got up; and a dead **dogmatism**[30], which **oppresses**[31], or raises opposition, will take the place of the lively confidence, born of personal conviction, which cheers and encourages the eminently sympathetic mind of childhood.

10. I have already hinted that such scientific training as we seek for may be given without making any extravagant claim upon the time now devoted to education. We ask only for "a most favoured nation" clause in our treaty with the schoolmaster; we demand no more than that science shall have as much time given to it as any other single subject—say four hours a week in each class of an ordinary school.

11. For the present, I think men of science would be well content with such an arrangement as this; but speaking for myself, I do not pretend to believe that such an arrangement can be, or will be, permanent. In these times the educational tree seems to me to have its roots in the air, its leaves and flowers in the ground; and, I confess, I should very much like to turn it upside down, so that its roots might be solidly embedded among the facts of Nature, and draw thence a sound **nutriment**[32] for the **foliage**[33] and fruit of literature and of art. No educational system can have a claim to permanence,

unless it recognizes the truth that education has two great ends to which everything else must be subordinated. The one of these is to increase knowledge; the other is to develop the love of right and the hatred of wrong.

12. With wisdom and uprightness a nation can make its way worthily, and beauty will follow in the footsteps of the two, even if she be not specially invited; while there is perhaps no sight in the whole world more saddening and revolting than is offered by men sunk in ignorance of everything but what other men have written; seemingly devoid of moral belief of guidance; but with the sense of beauty so keen, and the power of expression so cultivated, that their **sensual**[34] **caterwauling**[35] may be almost mistaken for the music of the spheres.

13. At present, education is almost entirely devoted to the cultivation of the power of expression, and of the sense of literary beauty. The matter of having anything to say, beyond a hash of other people's opinions, or of possessing any criterion of beauty, so that we may distinguish between the Godlike and the devilish, is left aside as of no moment. I think I do not err in saying that if science were made a foundation of education, instead of being, at most, stuck on as **cornice**[36] to the **edifice**[37], this state of things could not exist.

(From Thomas Henry Huxley's *Science and Education*)

Vocabulary

1. preparatory /prɪˈpærətri/

adj. for preparation 预备的；准备的

e. g. There is a lot of preparatory work involved in teaching.

2. modicum /ˈmɒdɪkəm/

n. a reasonable but not large amount(尤指好事或值得拥有的事物)少量；一点点

e. g. I'd like to think I've had a modicum of success.

3. peculiarity /pɪˌkjuːliˈærəti/

n. the quality of being peculiar 特性

e. g. Scientists tried to explain some peculiarities in the results of the experiment.

4. induction /ɪnˈdʌkʃn/

n. the use of individual ideas or facts to give you a general rule or conclusion 归纳；归纳法

5. deductive /dɪˈdʌktɪv/

adj. drawing conclusions logically from other things that are already known 推论的；演绎的

e. g. She didn't seem at all impressed by his deductive powers.

6. self-evident /ˌself ˈevɪdənt/

adj. so obvious that there is no need for proof or explanation 不证自明的；不言而喻的；明摆着的

e. g. It is self-evident that we will never have enough resources to meet the demand.

7. deduction /dɪˈdʌkʃn/

n. a conclusion that you have reached about something because of other things that you know to be true 推论；推断

e. g. My mother had consequently made her own shrewd deductions about what was going on in my marriage.

8. dispense with

stop using sb/sth because you no longer need them or it 摒弃；不再需要；不再用

e. g. No school is going to dispense with regulation.

9. apprehend /ˌæprɪˈhend/

v. understand fully 了解；明白

e. g. Only now can I begin to apprehend the power of these forces.

10. inductive /ɪnˈdʌktɪv/

adj. based on the process of induction 归纳法的；归纳的

11. at one's own peril

running the danger of oneself 危及自身

12. arbiter /ˈɑːbɪtə(r)/

n. a person or organization that has official power to settle disagreements 仲裁者；决定人

13. eminent /ˈemɪnənt/

adj. well-known and respected, especially because good at their profession（尤指因专业出众）著名的；受尊敬的；有声望的

e. g. He is eminent among scientists.

14. dissect /dɪˈsekt/

v. carefully cut something up in order to examine it scientifically 解剖（人体或动物躯体）

e. g. We dissected a frog in the biology class and we had learned a lot.

15. solicitous /səˈlɪsɪtəs/

adj. showing anxious concern for someone or something 关怀的；关切的；挂念的

e. g. He was so solicitous of his guests.

16. compel /kəmˈpel/

v. force someone to do something 强迫；逼迫

e. g. Leonie's mother was compelled to take in washing to help support her family.

17. conscientiously /ˌkɒnʃɪˈenʃəsli/

adv. carefully；diligently 尽责地；谨慎地；凭良心地

e. g. I carried out my duties conscientiously.

18. scanty /ˈskænti/

adj. lacking in amplitude or quantity 偏少的；不足的；欠缺的

e. g. So far, what scanty evidence we have points to two suspects.

19. commence /kəˈmens/

v. begin 开始

e. g. The academic year commences at the beginning of October.

20. Catechism /ˈkætəkɪzəm/

n. a series of questions and answers about religious beliefs, which has to be learned by people before they can become full members of that Church（天主教、圣公会或东正教的）教理问答；教义问答

21. comprehend /ˌkɒmprɪˈhend/

v. understand 理解；领悟

e. g. I just cannot comprehend your attitude.

22. incessantly /ɪnˈsesntli/

adv. without stopping 不间断地

23. stupidity /stjuːˈpɪdəti/

n. a lack of good judgment or intelligence 愚蠢；蠢事

e. g. I couldn't believe my own stupidity.

24. pedagogic /ˌpedəˈɡɒdʒɪk/

adj. concerning the methods and theory of teaching 教育的；教育方法的

e. g. Grammar is itself an ambiguous pedagogic concept.

25. repression /rɪˈpreʃn/

n. the use of force to restrict and control a society or other group of people 镇压；压制；控制

26. indigestible /ˌɪndɪˈdʒestəbl/

adj. difficult to understand, complicated, and dull 难理解的；难吸收的

e. g. Their presentation was an indigestible mass of information.

27. disposed /dɪˈspəʊzd/

adj. likely to behave or think in a particular way（态度、看法）有……倾向的

e. g. Many people seem disposed to distrust salespeople.

>>> Unit 7　Why Should Science Be Taught in Schools?

28. conviction /kənˈvɪkʃn/

n. great confidence in one's beliefs or opinions 坚信；深信；确信

e. g. She spoke with so much conviction that we all believed her.

29. phraseology /ˌfreɪziˈɒlədʒi/

n. words and expressions 用语；措辞

e. g. This careful phraseology is clearly intended to appeal to various sides of the conflict.

30. dogmatism /ˈdɒɡmətɪzəm/

n. the attitude of someone who is dogmatic 教条主义；武断；独断论

31. oppress /əˈpres/

v. treat cruelly or prevent from having the same opportunities, freedom, and benefits as others 压迫；压制

32. nutriment /ˈnjuːtrɪmənt/

n. a source of materials to nourish the body that can make people healthier 营养品；食物

33. foliage /ˈfəʊliɪdʒ/

n. the main organ of photosynthesis and transpiration in higher plants 树叶；植物

34. sensual /ˈsenʃuəl/

adj. of the appetites and passions of the body 感官的，肉欲的

35. caterwaul /ˈkætəwɔːl/

v. utter shrieks, as of cats 哀诉；抱怨；嚎叫

36. cornice /ˈkɔːnɪs/

n. a molding at the corner between the ceiling and the top of a wall 飞檐；上楣

37. edifice /ˈedɪfɪs/

n. a structure that has a roof and walls and stands more or less permanently in one place 大厦；大建筑物

Exercises for Text 2

I. Decide whether the statements are true (T) or false (F) according to the text.

1. Scientific education in whatever form will be better than sticking to teaching the Latin Grammar.
2. Mathematical training is almost purely inductive.
3. You cannot make a boy see the battle of Thermopylae for himself or observe the scene where Cromwell ruled England.
4. As soon as it is fit for systematic instruction of any kind, it is fit for teaching a little bit science.

5. When teachers teach kids botany, they must let those kids handle the plants and dissect the flowers for themselves.

II. Translate the following sentences with the key words in the parentheses.

1. 在开始动工之前,至少需要做一年的准备工作。(preparatory)
2. 经济大萧条对该国的影响是显而易见的。(self-evident)
3. 地方福利部门就是政府贯彻实施其众多服务的窗口。(dispense)
4. 他们开始进行彻底搜查。(commence)
5. 每当她听不懂的时候,她总是会笑。(comprehend)
6. 我们不能允许教条主义阻碍进步。(dogmatism)
7. 让她心烦的不只是天气。(oppress)
8. 她的行动是出于虔诚的宗教信仰。(conviction)
9. 我觉得必须写信告诉你,我非常欣赏你的书。(compel)
10. 可获得的极少数资料,大多来自中国的记载。(scanty)

III. Explain the following sentences in your own words.

1. But this modicum of instruction must be so given as to ensure real knowledge and practical discipline.
2. If scientific education is to be dealt with as mere bookwork, it will be better not to attempt it, but to stick to the Latin Grammar which makes no pretense to be anything but bookwork.
3. The great peculiarity of scientific training, that in virtue of which it cannot be replaced by any other discipline whatsoever, is this bringing of the mind directly into contact with fact, and practicing the intellect in the completest form of induction.
4. And, especially, tell him that it is his duty to doubt until he is compelled, by the absolute authority of Nature, to believe that which is written in books.
5. Pursue this discipline carefully and conscientiously, and you may make sure that, however scanty may be the measure of information which you have poured into the boy's mind, you have created an intellectual habit of priceless value in practical life.

>>> Unit 7　Why Should Science Be Taught in Schools?

Learning Strategies

Learning Vocabulary through Roots

Remembering roots is a very effective way to understand and memorize words. Roots can make seemingly difficult long words easier because the long words become a meaningful combination of several roots and affixes which all have their own meanings. In this unit we can find lots of words which can be remembered by understanding the roots. For example,

- Gratification, "grat" means "pleasing". More examples: gratify; gratifying ...
- Compel, "pel" means "to push". More examples: repel; dispel ...
- Deduction, "duct" means "to lead". More examples: induction; conductor ...
- Pedagogic, "ped" means "children". More examples: pedagogy; pedophile ...

Now you can find more words that can be understood by identifying their roots.

Unit Project

Work in groups to make research on articles about the importance of science and make a presentation about it for 10 minutes.
1. Find articles about the importance of science and sum up their views.
2. Hold a discussion in groups about whether you agree with the views of those articles.
3. Give an analysis of those articles by using Spenser's and Hutching's view.
4. Make a presentation to your classmates.

Unit 8

Life as Education

Pre-reading questions:

1. For Spenser, the aim of education is the preparation of "complete life", then what is the aim of education according to John Dewey?
2. What do you know about the educational idea—"Life is education"?

>>> Unit 8 Life as Education

Text 1
The Conception of Educational Development

John Dewey

1. We have had so far but little to say in this chapter about education. We have been **occupied**¹ with the conditions and **implications**² of growth. If our conclusions are justified, they carry with them, however, definite educational consequences. When it is said that education is development, everything depends upon how development is conceived. Our net conclusion is that life is development, and that developing, growing, is life. Translated into its educational equivalents, this means (ⅰ) that the educational process has no end beyond itself; it is its own end; and that (ⅱ) the educational process is one of continual reorganizing, reconstructing, transforming.

2. Development when it is interpreted in comparative terms, that is, with respect to the special **traits**³ of child and adult life, means the direction of power into special channels: the formation of habits involving executive skill, definiteness of interest, and specific objects of observation and thought. But the comparative view is not final. The child has specific powers; to ignore that fact is to **stunt**⁴ or **distort**⁵ the organs upon which his growth depends. The adult uses his powers to transform his environment, thereby **occasioning**⁶ new stimuli which redirect his powers and keep them developing. Ignoring this fact means arrested development, a passive accommodation. Normal child and normal adult alike, in other words, are engaged in growing. The difference between them is not the difference between growth and no growth, but between the modes of growth appropriate to different conditions. With respect to the development of powers devoted to coping with specific scientific and economic problems we may say the child should be growing in manhood. With respect to sympathetic curiosity, unbiased responsiveness, and openness of mind, we may say that the adult should be growing in childlikeness. One statement is as true as the other.

3. Three ideas which have been criticized, namely, the merely privative nature of immaturity, static adjustment to a fixed environment, and **rigidity**[7] of habit, are all connected with a false idea of growth or development—that it is a movement toward a fixed goal. Growth is regarded as having an end, instead of being an end. The educational **counterparts**[8] of the three **fallacious**[9] ideas are first, failure to take account of the instinctive or native powers of the young; secondly, failure to develop initiative in coping with novel situations; thirdly, an **undue**[10] emphasis upon drill and other devices which secure automatic skill at the expense of perception. In all cases, the adult environment is accepted as a standard for the child. He is to be brought up to it.

4. Natural instincts are either **disregarded**[11] or treated as **nuisances**[12]—as **obnoxious**[13] traits to be **suppressed**[14], or at all events to be brought into **conformity**[15] with external standards. Since conformity is the aim, what is distinctively individual in a young person is brushed aside, or regarded as a source of mischief or **anarchy**[16]. Conformity is made equivalent to uniformity. Consequently, there are induced lack of interest in the novel, **aversion**[17] to progress, and **dread**[18] of the uncertain and the unknown. Since the end of growth is outside of and beyond the process of growing, external agents have to be resorted to **induce**[19] movement towards it. Whenever a method of education is **stigmatized**[20] as mechanical, we may be sure that external pressure is brought to bear to reach an external end.

5. Since in reality there is nothing to which growth is relative **save**[21] more growth, there is nothing to which education is subordinate save more education. It is a commonplace to say that education should not cease when one leaves school. The point of this commonplace is that the purpose of school education is to ensure the continuance of life by organizing the powers that ensure growth. The inclination to learn from life itself and to make the conditions of life such that all will learn in the process of living is the finest product of schooling.

6. When we abandon the attempt to define immaturity by means of fixed comparison with adult accomplishments, we are **compelled**[22] to give up thinking of it as **denoting**[23] lack of desired traits. Abandoning this **notion**[24], we are also forced to surrender our habit of thinking of instruction as a method of supplying this lack by pouring knowledge into a mental and moral hole

which awaits filling. Since life means growth, a living creature lives as truly and positively at one stage as at another, with the same **intrinsic**[25] fullness and the same absolute claims. Hence education means the enterprise of supplying the conditions which insure growth, or **adequacy**[26] of life, **irrespective of**[27] age. We first look with impatience upon immaturity, regarding it as something to be got over as rapidly as possible. Then the adult formed by such educative methods looks back with impatient regret upon childhood and youth as a scene of lost opportunities and wasted powers. This ironical situation will endure till it is recognized that living has its own intrinsic quality and that the business of education is with that quality.

7. Realization that life is growth protects us from that so-called idealizing of childhood which in effect is nothing but lazy **indulgence**[28]. Life is not to be identified with every superficial act and interest. Even though it is not always easy to tell whether what appears to be mere surface fooling is a sign of some **nascent**[29] as yet untrained power, we must remember that manifestations are not to be accepted as ends in themselves. They are signs of possible growth. They are to be turned into means of development, of carrying power forward, not **indulged**[30] or cultivated for their own sake. Excessive attention to surface phenomena (even in the way of **rebuke**[31] as well as of encouragement) may lead to their **fixation**[32] and thus to **arrested**[33] development. What impulses are moving toward, not what they have been, is the important thing for parent and teacher. The true principle of respect for immaturity cannot be better put than in the words of Emerson: "Respect the child. Be not too much his parent. **Trespass**[34] not on his **solitude**[35]. But I hear the **outcry**[36] which replies to this suggestion: would you **verily**[37] throw up the reins of public and private discipline; would you leave the young child to the mad career of his own passions and **whimsies**[38], and call this anarchy a respect for the child's nature? I answer—respect the child, respect him to the end, but also respect yourself …

8. The three points in a boy's training are: to keep his nature and train off all but that; to keep his nature, but stop off his **uproar**[39], fooling, and **horseplay**[40]; to keep his nature and arm it with knowledge in the very direction in which it points. And as Emerson goes on to show this **reverence**[41] for childhood and youth instead of opening up an easy and easy-going path to the instructor, "involves at once, immense claims on the time,

the thought, on the life of the teacher. It requires time, use, insight, event, all the great lessons and assistances of God; and only to think of using it implies character and profoundness."

(From John Dewey's *Democracy and Education*)

Vocabulary

1. occupied /ˈɒkjupaɪd/

adj. busy doing or thinking about 忙于

2. implication /ˌɪmplɪˈkeɪʃn/

n. the things that are likely to happen as a result; what statement, event, or situation implies or suggests 可能引发的后果;暗示;含意

e. g. The Attorney General was aware of the political implications of his decision to prosecute.

The implication was obvious: vote for us or it will be very embarrassing for you.

3. trait /treɪt/

n. a particular characteristic, quality, or tendency that someone or something has 特征;特点

e. g. Creativity is a human trait.

4. stunt /stʌnt/

v. prevent something from growing or developing as much as it should 阻碍(生长);妨碍(发展)

e. g. The heart condition had stunted his growth a bit.

5. distort /dɪˈstɔːt/

v. report or represent in an untrue way 歪曲;扭曲;曲解

e. g. The media distorts reality, categorizing people as all good or all bad.

6. occasion /əˈkeɪʒn/

v. cause 导致;引起

e. g. He argued that the release of hostages should not occasion a change in policy.

7. rigidity /rɪˈdʒɪdəti/

n. the physical property of being stiff and resisting bending 严格;坚硬

8. counterpart /ˈkaʊntəpɑːt/

n. another person or thing that has a similar function or position in a different place 职能（或地位）相当的人；对应的事物

e. g. The Foreign Secretary telephoned his Italian counterpart to protest. They had big arguments.

9. **fallacious** /fəˈleɪʃəs/

adj. wrong because based on a fallacy 谬误的；错误的

e. g. Their main argument is fallacious.

10. **undue** /ˌʌnˈdjuː/

adj. greater or more extreme than reasonable or appropriate 过分的；过度的

e. g. This would help the families to survive the drought without undue suffering.

11. **disregard** /ˌdɪsrɪˈɡɑːd/

v. ignore or do not take account of 不理会；不顾

e. g. He disregarded the advice of his executives.

12. **nuisance** /ˈnjuːsns/

n. somebody or something that annoys you or causes you a lot of problems 讨厌的人；麻烦的事情

e. g. He could be a bit of a nuisance when he was drunk.

13. **obnoxious** /əbˈnɒkʃəs/

adj. very unpleasant 令人讨厌的；使人反感的

e. g. He was an obnoxious person. No one liked him.

14. **suppress** /səˈpres/

v. stop something from continuing or developing 压制；抑制；阻止

15. **conformity** /kənˈfɔːməti/

n. the state of happening as the law says or as the person wants it to; the state of behaving in the same way as most other people （对法律、个人意愿等的）遵从；遵守；墨守成规；循规蹈矩

e. g. Was his action in conformity with the law?
Excessive conformity is usually caused by fear of disapproval.

16. **anarchy** /ˈænəki/

n. state where nobody seems to be paying any attention to rules or laws 无政府（状态）；无秩序

e. g. Civil war and famine sent the nation plunging into anarchy.

17. **aversion** /əˈvɜːʃn/

n. a feeling of intense dislike 厌恶；讨厌；反感

e. g. He seems to have an aversion to exercise.

18. **dread** /dred/

n. the feeling of anxiety and unhappiness about something which is unpleasant or upsetting 担心；害怕

e. g. The prospect of growing old fills me with dread.

19. induce /ɪnˈdjuːs/

v. cause 引起；导致

e. g. Doctors said surgery could induce a heart attack.

20. stigmatize /ˈstɪɡmətaɪz/

v. unfairly regard something as being bad or have something to be ashamed of 侮辱；污蔑；使蒙羞

e. g. The AIDS epidemic further stigmatized gays.

21. save /seɪv/

prep. except 除了

e. g. They knew nothing about her save her name.

22. compel /kəmˈpel/

v. force someone to do something 强迫；逼迫

e. g. The introduction of legislation to compel cyclists to wear a helmet was understood by people at last.

23. denote /dɪˈnəʊt/

v. be a sign or indication of something 预示；是……的征兆；是……的标志

e. g. Red eyes denote strain and fatigue.

24. notion /ˈnəʊʃn/

n. an idea or belief about something 看法；观念

e. g. We each have a notion of just what kind of person we'd like to be.

25. intrinsic /ɪnˈtrɪnzɪk, ɪnˈtrɪnsɪk/

adj. valuable or interesting because of the basic nature or character 内在的；本身的；固有的

e. g. The intrinsic value of education has been universally recognized.

26. adequacy /ˈædɪkwəsi/

n. the quality of being good enough or great enough in amount to be acceptable 适当；恰当

e. g. He doubted her adequacy for the job.

27. irrespective of

not affected or should not be affected by something 不考虑……的；不顾……的

e. g. This service should be available to everybody, irrespective of whether they can afford it.

28. indulgence /ɪnˈdʌldʒəns/

n. the act of treating someone with special kindness, often when it is not a good thing 纵容；迁就

e. g. The king's indulgence towards his sons angered the business community.

29. nascent /ˈnæsnt/

adj. beginning or formed recently 新兴的；新生的

>>> Unit 8 Life as Education

e.g. The smartwatch market is still nascent, so it is reasonable to invest in the market.

30. indulge /ɪnˈdʌldʒ/

v. allow oneself to have or do something that they know they will enjoy; let someone have or do what they want, even if this is not good for them （使自己）沉迷；放纵（自己）；纵容；迁就；娇惯

e.g. Only rarely will she indulge in a glass of wine.

He did not agree with indulging children.

31. rebuke /rɪˈbjuːk/

v. speak severely to others because they have said or done something that someone does not approve of 指责；非难；谴责

e.g. The company was publicly rebuked for having neglected safety procedures.

32. fixation /fɪkˈseɪʃn/

n. the act of thinking about a particular subject or person to an extreme and excessive degree 迷恋；痴迷

33. arrest /əˈrest/

v. stop something continuing 阻止；抑制

e.g. The sufferer may have to make major changes in his or her life to arrest the disease.

34. trespass /ˈtrespəs/

v. involve oneself in something that is not their concern 干涉；妨碍；插手

e.g. He told me I was trespassing on private land.

35. solitude /ˈsɒlɪtjuːd/

n. the state of being alone, especially when this is peaceful and pleasant（尤指平静愉快的）独居；独处

e.g. She longed for peace and solitude.

36. outcry /ˈaʊtkraɪ/

n. a reaction of strong disapproval and anger shown by the public or media about a recent event 强烈的抗议（或反对）

e.g. The killing caused an international outcry.

37. verily /ˈverɪli/

adv. an old-fashioned or religious word meaning "truly" 真实地；确实

e.g. Verily I say unto you, that one of you shall betray me.

38. whimsy /ˈwɪmzi/

n. behaviour which is unusual, playful, and unpredictable, rather than having any serious reason or purpose behind it 奇思异想；不同寻常的行为

e.g. He had a whimsy about flying to the moon.

141

39. uproar /ˈʌprɔː(r)/

n. a lot of shouting and noise because people are very angry or upset about something 喧闹；吵闹；鼓噪；骚动

e. g. The announcement caused uproar in the crowd.

40. horseplay /ˈhɔːspleɪ/

n. rough play in which people push and hit each other, or behave in a silly way 动手动脚的嬉戏；打闹

41. reverence /ˈrevərəns/

n. a feeling of great respect for something 尊敬；崇敬；敬意

e. g. They show a deep reverence for their religion.

Exercises for Text 1

I. Read the text and answer the questions.

1. What is the relationship between development and life?
2. What is the difference between children's growth and adults' growth?
3. What are the three wrong ideas about education?
4. How should we look at immaturity?
5. How should we respect children?

II. Complete the sentences with the words below. Change the form where necessary.

disregard	aversion	obnoxious	induce	arrest
conformity	counterpart	notion	distort	undue
stigmatize	stunt	implication	intrinsic	uproar
compel	bearing	denote	trait	outcry

1. My father's achievements really don't have any _____ on what I do. I have to depend on myself.
2. The low level of current investment has serious _____ for future economic growth. It might slow down the economic growth.
3. The study found that some alcoholics had clear personality _____ showing up early in childhood. For example, they did not have strong self-control.
4. High interest rates have _____ economic growth. Many economists are worried about the slow growth.
5. The minister has said his remarks at the weekend have been _____, which has made many people misunderstand him.
6. The Foreign Minister held talks with his Chinese _____. The two ministers were both satisfied with the meeting.

>>> Unit 8 Life as Education

7. We did not want to put any _____ pressure on them. They had already been under pressure.
8. Safety rules were _____, which led to the accident.
9. The people at my table were so _____ I simply had to change my seat.
10. _____ with people around us is usually caused by fear. We are afraid that we will be isolated if we are different from others.
11. Many people have a natural and emotional _____ to insects.
12. It was an economic crisis _____ by high oil prices.
13. Children in single-parent families must not be _____. They should be given respect and understanding.
14. Leonie's mother was _____ to do the job she didn't like in order to help support her family.
15. There was a message waiting, _____ that someone had been here ahead of her.
16. I reject absolutely the _____ that privatisation of our industry is now inevitable.
17. The process attribute is a(n) _____ attribute of the curriculum. The process is highly valued in this curriculum.
18. The drug was used to _____ the spread of the disease. Now as expected, the disease was successfully eliminated by the drug.
19. The new tax provoked a public _____. People thought it was too heavy.
20. The audience burst into a(n) _____ when they found the two famous actors were really fighting with each other on the stage.

III. Translate the sentences into Chinese.

1. If our conclusions are justified, they carry with them, however, definite educational consequences.
2. Development when it is interpreted in comparative terms, that is, with respect to the special traits of child and adult life, means the direction of power into special channels.
3. To ignore that fact is to stunt or distort the organs upon which his growth depends.
4. Would you leave the young child to the mad career of his own passions and whimsies, and call this anarchy a respect for the child's nature?
5. Since life means growth, a living creature lives as truly and positively at one stage as at another, with the same intrinsic fullness and the same absolute claims.

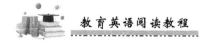

Text 2

Creative Education

Tao Xingzhi

The Primary School is the foundation of all education. The **conception**[1] of the educational process has changed greatly through the years.

I. School and Society

1. At first school and society were entirely separate; more recently society was brought into the school. This was like bringing a beautiful bird into a cage so as to enjoy it and watch it.

2. Lately we have begun to take the school into society. The school is poor; it uses society as its school room and becomes rich. By taking the school into society, using the community as the school room, the educational process becomes: first, Rich; second, Natural; third, Real; fourth, Economical; fifth, in Harmony with the Progress of Society.

3. It does not go ahead too fast, nor **lag**[2] behind. To invite a vocational teacher to come to the school is very expensive; to go to the industries of the community to learn gets better results and these results are all real and practical.

II. Education and Life

1. In the first stage of man's life education and life were one and the same, but as the need for formal schools **arose**[3] they became separated.

2. Later, it was said, "Education is life." Education tried to bring as much of life as possible into the school.

3. I believe that life is education. The kind of education you receive depends on the kind of life you live. **Hygiene**[4] text books and living **hygienically**[5] are two things. Therefore, we will get our education while we are living.

III. Education and Method

1. For many years, education was giving knowledge to the student;

later, education was teaching the student to learn; still more recently, education is teaching the student how to work. This brings about a unity, in teaching, learning, acting. The method of acting determines the method of learning; the method of learning determines the method of teaching.

2. Creative education is the result of this method. Creative education means a **transfusion**[6] of energy in the creation of a new order. It will imply that the whole of society is a school—not a room and 42 benches.

3. There are five steps in Dewey's **reflective**[7] thinking:

1) The feeling of difficulty.

2) The location of difficulty.

3) The proposed solution.

4) The selection of one solution for trial.

5) After repeated trials, **verify**[8] the results.

4. This philosophy came to China fifteen years ago, and was received with joy. Chinese scholars welcomed reflective thinking, so people just sat and thought. They recognized the difficulties and thought about them. They were difficulties felt through books and lectures. These difficulties were **manufactured**[9] in our heads. I propose to add one step before the feeling of difficulties. The first step should be action. Then the other five may follow and they will lead to more action. So education should begin with action. Then difficulties will be real, not felt simply through book knowledge, lectures, facts and figures, but experienced through action and followed by reflective thinking.

5. I would give a new name to the whole: "Reflective action". Action will connect ideas and motor **fibers**[10] and the electric **current**[11] will come through. Reflective activity implies action of both brain and hands. We no longer have a class in society for hands, another class with head. All are hands and head.

IV. Education and the Masses

1. In early education, ears and mouth only were used. The result was about inches of education, the distance between the ear and the mouth.

2. Later, eyes, ears and mouth were used. Chinese education is now in this **triangular**[12] stage.

3. In the new education, hands and brain are connected. Action and thinking must progress together. **Coolies**[13] use only action; **intellectuals**[14] use only brains; both lead to defeat. Using both together leads to progress

and invention.

4. There are two approaches to this **universal**[15] education: (a) teach farmers and workers to use their heads, (b) teach scholars and students to use their hands. The electrical lamps that shine upon us were built by thinking and experiment, step by step. They are the results of applied thinking. Reflective activity always brings invention. If brains and hands come together, there will be a new civilization. By bringing both hands and head, a new world will be created.

5. Two treasures with us lifelong remain,

A pair of free hands and a great brain;

He who doesn't use his hands

Belongs to the **dethroned**[16] King's bands.

He who doesn't use his brain

Has to **endure**[17] hunger and pain.

He who uses both brain and hand

Can set up Heaven's kingdom on Satan's land.

V. Education and the Student

1. We have to begin this process in childhood. My children do this better than I do. Take the children out of the **amah's**[18] hands. **Cast**[19] out of them all fears. Then children will be little workers and teachers, the directors of work. Each will have a share in creation and be a creator.

2. The new school is not just a school; neither is it a factory. It is a place for **collective**[20] living, a community. It is shop, school, and life. The school doesn't depend upon buildings, expensive equipment, wide playground. Every occupation uses sciences, hands and brain. Let the children use occupation as their school, and learn by working as workers, thinkers and creators.

3. We cannot create a new China and hand it down to future generations. We must educate the children and give them from the beginning their part in the creation of a new world.

4. It is the doer rather than the enjoyer who gets the education. Those who do must learn to enjoy; those who enjoy must learn to do.

5. These are some of the proposals which I make to Chinese education.

(From Tao Xingzhi's *Education for Life*)

Vocabulary

1. conception /kənˈsepʃn/

n. an idea that someone has in their mind 概念；观念；想法

e.g. My conception of a garden was based on gardens I had visited in England.

2. lag /læg/

v. progress more slowly than that of the other 落后；赶不上

e.g. We still lag far behind many of our competitors in using modern technology.

3. arise /əˈraɪz/

v. begin to exist 发生；出现

e.g. If a problem arises later in the pregnancy, it will be very harmful.

4. hygiene /ˈhaɪdʒiːn/

n. the practice of keeping oneself and one's surroundings clean, especially in order to prevent illness or the spread of diseases（尤指为防止患病或疾病传播的）卫生

e.g. Be extra careful about personal hygiene.

5. hygienically /haɪˈdʒiːnɪkli/

adv. in a hygienic manner 卫生地

6. transfusion /trænsˈfjuːʒn/

n. the introduction of blood or blood plasma into a vein or artery; the action of pouring a liquid from one vessel to another 输血；渗透

e.g. Without a transfusion, the victim's probability of dying was 100%.

7. reflective /rɪˈflektɪv/

adj. thinking deeply about something 沉思的；反思的

e.g. Mike is a quiet and reflective man.

8. verify /ˈverɪfaɪ/

v. check that it is true by careful examination or investigation; state or confirm that it is true 核实；查证；查清；证实；证明

e.g. A clerk simply verifies that the payment and invoice amount match.

The government has not verified any of those reports.

9. manufacture /ˌmænjuˈfæktʃə(r)/

v. invent information that is not true 虚构；捏造

e.g. He said the allegations were manufactured on little evidence.

10. fiber /ˈfaɪbə/

n. a slender and greatly elongated solid substance 纤维

11. **current** /ˈkʌrənt/

n. a flow of electricity through a wire or circuit 电流

12. **triangular** /traɪˈæŋɡjələ(r)/

adj. involving three people or things 三角关系的；三人间的；三方面的

13. **coolie** /ˈkuːli/

n. an offensive name for an unskilled Asian laborer 苦力

14. **intellectual** /ˌɪntəˈlektʃuəl/

n. someone who spends a lot of time studying and thinking about complicated ideas 知识分子；脑力劳动者

15. **universal** /ˌjuːnɪˈvɜːsl/

adj. relating to everyone in the world or everyone in a particular group or society 普遍的；全体的

e. g. The desire to look attractive is universal.

16. **dethrone** /ˌdiːˈθrəʊn/

v. remove from the position of power 废黜；罢免

e. g. He was dethroned and went into exile.

17. **endure** /ɪnˈdjʊə(r)/

v. not avoid or give up, usually because you cannot 忍耐；忍受

e. g. They had to endure unbearable pain in solitude because not even the doctors could get near them.

18. **amah** /ˈɑːmə/

n. a woman employed by a family to clean, care for children, etc 奶妈；保姆

19. **cast** /kɑːst/

v. throw 扔；抛；投；丢

e. g. In Armenia, people can cast small coins to the bride.

20. **collective** /kəˈlektɪv/

adj. shared by every member of a group of people 集体的；共同的

e. g. It was a collective decision.

Exercises for Text 2

I. Decide whether the statements are true (T) or false (F) according to the text.

1. There are six steps in Dewey's reflective thinking.

2. We can let children create. For example, we can let them be little workers and teachers.
3. We need to teach farmers to use their hands and scholars to use their heads.
4. Reflective activity will not bring invention.
5. The new school should be both a school and a factory.

II. Translate the following sentences with the key words in the parentheses.

1. 我认为他丝毫没有团队意识。(conception)
2. 我的思想落后于现实。(lag)
3. 一有机会,鸟儿们也会破坏庄稼。(arise)
4. 我心事重重地向车子走去。(reflective)
5. 我核实了我所获消息的来源。(verify)
6. 根据控方意见,他们精心编造了事情经过。(manufacture)
7. 保险业提出了自己的全民医疗保健方案。(universal)
8. 那家公司遭受了严重亏损。(endure)
9. 只要你心诚,往喷泉里扔下一根大头针,然后盯着泉水看,就能看见未来伴侣的影子。(cast)
10. 我确实深深地感受到集体的力量。(collective)

III. Explain the following sentences in your own words.

1. At first school and society were entirely separate; more recently society was brought into the school.
2. To invite a vocational teacher to come to the school is very expensive; to go to the industries of the community to learn gets better results and these results are all real and practical.
3. The method of acting determines the method of learning; the method of learning determines the method of teaching.
4. Action will connect ideas and motor fibers and the electric current will come through.
5. Reflective activity always brings invention. If brains and hands come together, there will be built a new civilization.

Learning Strategies

Skimming

Skimming means reading the text quickly to get the main idea.

When skimming, read the title, the main headings, the first and last paragraphs, and the first sentence of each paragraph. This will give you a good idea of what the text is about.

For example, when we see the heading "School and Society", the first sentence and the last sentence in Part I of the second text, we know this part is about the relationship between school and society.

Now find an article by yourself and try to predict the main idea of the text according to the heading (if any), the first sentence and the last sentence.

Unit Project

Work in groups to make research on articles about the idea of "life is education" and write a report about this.

1. Find articles talking about the tenet of "life is education".
2. Design a questionnaire about this tenet.
3. Conduct an investigation about your classmates' views on this by using the questionnaire.
4. Write a report of 800 words about this.

>>> Unit 9 Punishments and Rewards

Unit 9
Punishments and Rewards

Pre-reading questions:

1. What do you know about Percy Nunn's ideas about how to discipline children?
2. What is the principle of punishing children?

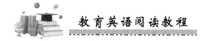

READING & CRITICAL THINKING

Text 1

The Way to Discipline Kids

Thomas Percy Nunn

1. Thus we reach once more the principle that the proper aim of education is **positive**[1], to encourage free activity, not **negative**[2], to confine or to **repress**[3] it. What becomes, then, of the concept of discipline which is so essential in the traditional ideas about school training? To gain a clear answer to this question, we must first distinguish between discipline and school order, and see that though they **overlap**[4] and indeed **interpenetrate**[5] they are derived from quite different psychological roots. School order consists in the maintenance of the conditions necessary if school life is to fulfill its purpose, and, as we saw, is most effective when based on imitation and the routine tendency. Discipline, on the other hand, is not an **external**[6] thing, like order, but something that touches the **inmost**[7] springs of conduct. It consists in the **submission**[8] of one's impulses and powers to a regulation which imposes form upon their chaos, and brings efficiency and economy where there would otherwise be ineffectiveness and waste. Though parts of our nature may resist this control, its acceptance must, on the whole, be willing acceptance—the spontaneous movement of a nature in which there is an inborn impulse towards greater perfection or "expressiveness".

2. Thus the process of discipline is **akin**[9] to **consolidation**[10]; it may, in fact, be regarded as a higher type of consolidation, differing from the lower type in that it involves some degree of conscious purpose. We may properly speak of the movements of an athlete as disciplined; for they have gained their perfect form and efficiency—in a word, their expressiveness—largely through conscious effort. Similarly, we may speak of a person as disciplined by circumstances when he has deliberately used the lessons of hard experience to give shape to his impulses and powers. But though a person may discipline himself as those do who rise to greatness in spite of hostile circumstance,

yet discipline is, in general, the influence of a wider or better organized mind upon one narrower or less developed. In all cases there is, in a disciplinary process, a definite psychological sequence. First, there must be something that one **genuinely**[11] desires to do, and one must be conscious either of one's inability or of someone else's superior ability to do it. Next, the **perception**[12] of **inferiority**[13] must awaken the negative self-feeling with its impulse to fix attention upon the points in which one's own performance falls short or the models excels. Lastly, comes the repetition of efforts, controlled now by a better concept of the proper procedure, and accompanied, if successful, by an **outflow**[14] of positive self-feeling which tends to make the improved **schema**[15] **permanent**[16].

3. We can hardly leave the subject of discipline without some reference to the place of punishment in the school economy. Here the essential point to seize is that the intention of punishment should be positive, not negative; it should aim at helping the **backslider**[17] to do willingly what he ought to do, rather than at preventing him from doing what is forbidden. Even in the treatment of crime it is now well established—though the fruits of the discovery are sadly slow in maturing—that mere **repression**[18] is no cure, and that the true remedy lies in the "**sublimation**"[19] of the criminal's misdirected energies. Punishment may properly be used as a **deterrent**[20] against acts, such as **unpunctuality**[21] and disobedience, that clearly violate the school order which it is the common interest to maintain. But it has no moral effect unless approved by the general sense of the community. Disorderly and other mildly anti-social acts are often best punished by mere exclusion of the offender from the common occupation; the sight of other children happily busy while he is reduced to **nauseous**[22] inactivity wakens the strongest **motive**[23] to **repentance**[24]. This principle does not, however, justify the **pernicious**[25] practice of "keeping in" children whose naughtiness is an **irritability**[26] due to boredom, to insufficient sleep, or lack of fresh air or exercise; to cut such a child off from his play is to **withhold**[27] the specific **remedy**[28] for his disease. In proportion as an offence assumes the character of a sin, the deterrent and **retributive**[29] aspects of punishment should become entirely subordinate to the **remedial**[30]. It should look not towards the unsatisfactory past, but towards the still hopeful **fixture**[31]. One may feel shame when made to see oneself in

the unpleasant character in which one appears to others, but a real "change of heart" comes only as one secures hold on a better way of life. The wise teacher, then, will not be **contented**[32] merely to repress the symptoms of spiritual sickness, but will try by all possible means to remove its causes. And, as we have seen, those causes always consist in the disorderly, **mal-adjusted**[33] working of impulses—attraction and **repulsions**[34], conscious, and still more frequently unconscious—which by **prudent**[35] handling may be redirected into the ways of spiritual health.

4. To these few observations we add only one general remark. The conviction, once so deeply rooted in the teaching profession, that punishment and the fear of punishment are the natural foundations of school government, is gradually being recognized as merely a **barbarous**[36] **superstition**[37]. Every teacher of wide experience now knows that a school in whose atmosphere the thunder clouds of punishment are always **brooding**[38] may often show no superiority, as regards visible order, over one where punishment is a **rarity**[39]. Offences must come and must be dealt with, but it is a sound principle to regard them, in general, as signs of **mal-adjustment**[40] rather than of natural wickedness; that is, to take them as indications that there is something wrong in the curriculum, the methods of instruction, or in the physical or spiritual conditions of the school work and life.

5. From the general **tenor**[41] of our argument throughout the book it is clear that while the school must be a society, it must be a society of a special character. It must be a natural society, in the sense that there should be no violent break between the conditions of life within and without it. There should be no **cramping**[42] or **stifling**[43] of the citizen's energies, but room for everyone to live wholly and **vigorously**[44]; no **conventional**[45] standards of conduct, but only the universal **canons**[46] and ideals; no academic separation from the interests of the great world, but a hearty participation in them. On the other hand, a school must be an artificial society in the sense that while it should reflect the outer world truly, it should reflect only what is best and most vital there. A nation's schools, we might say, are an organ of its life, whose special function is to consolidate its spiritual strength, to maintain its historic continuity, to secure its past achievements, to guarantee its future. Through its schools a nation should become conscious of the **abiding**[47]

>>> Unit 9　Punishments and Rewards

sources from which the best movements in its life have always drawn their inspiration, should constantly **submit**[48] itself to self-criticism, should **purge**[49] its ideals, should reinform and redirect its impulses.

(From Thomas Percy Nunn's *Education: Its Data and First Principles*)

Vocabulary

1. positive /ˈpɒzətɪv/

adj. indicating agreement, approval, or encouragement 积极的；肯定的

e. g. There's been a positive response to the UN Secretary-General's recent peace efforts.

2. negative /ˈneɡətɪv/

adj. considering only the bad aspects of a situation, rather than the good ones 消极的；悲观的

e. g. When asked for your views about your current job, on no account must you be negative about it.

3. repress /rɪˈpres/

v. restrict freedom 压制；限制（自由）

e. g. People who repress their emotions risk having nightmares.

4. overlap /ˌəʊvəˈlæp, ˈəʊvəlæp/

v. involve some of the same subjects, people, or periods of time（在主题、人物、时间等上）（与……）部分相同；（与……）部分交叉

e. g. Our jobs overlap slightly, which sometimes causes difficulties.

5. interpenetrate /ˌɪntəˈpenɪtreɪt/

v. penetrate mutually or be interlocked 渗透；互相贯通

6. external /ɪkˈstɜːnl/

adj. on the outside of a surface or body, or existing, happening, or coming from outside 外部的；外面的；外来的

e. g. A combination of internal and external factors caused the company to close down.

7. inmost /ˈɪnməʊst/

adj. innermost 内心最深处的

155

e. g. He knew in his inmost heart that he was behaving badly. So he had great regrets about it.

8. submission /səbˈmɪʃn/

n. a state in which people can no longer do what they want to do because they have been brought under the control of someone else 屈服；投降；归顺；顺服

e. g. The army intends to take the city or simply starve it into submission.

9. akin /əˈkɪn/

adj. similar to in some way 相似的；类似的

e. g. Listening to his life story is akin to reading a good adventure novel.

10. consolidation /kənˌsɒlɪˈdeɪʃən/

n. the act of strengthening something so that it becomes more effective or secure 加强；巩固

e. g. The change has brought about the growth and consolidation of the middle class.

11. genuinely /ˈdʒenjuɪnli/

adv. in real and not pretended manner 真挚地；真诚地

e. g. He genuinely cares about his employees.

12. perception /pəˈsepʃn/

n. the way that you think about something or the impression you have of something 理解；看法；认识

e. g. He is interested in how our perceptions of death affect the way we live.

13. inferiority /ɪnˌfɪərɪˈɒrəti/

n. the state of being inferior 劣势；下等；自卑

14. outflow /ˈaʊtfləʊ/

n. the movement of a large amount of money or people from one place to another（金钱、人等的）外流；流出

e. g. There was a net outflow of about ￡50 m in short-term capital.

15. schema /ˈskiːmə/

n. a conception of what is common to all members of a class; a mental model of aspects of the world or of the self that is structured in such a way as to facilitate the processes of cognition and perception 心理模式；图式；框架

16. permanent /ˈpɜːmənənt/

adj. lasting forever 永久的；永恒的

e. g. Heavy drinking can cause permanent damage to the brain.

17. backslider /ˈbækslaɪdə/

n. someone who lapses into previous undesirable patterns of behavior 故态复萌的人；更改一段时间后又恢复旧习惯者

>>> Unit 9　Punishments and Rewards

18. **repression** /rɪˈpreʃn/

n. unwillingness to allow oneself to have natural feelings and desires 压抑；控制

19. **sublimation** /ˌsʌblɪˈmeɪʃn/

n. the act of expressing something in a way that is socially acceptable 升华；高尚化

20. **deterrent** /dɪˈterənt/

n. something that prevents people from doing something by making them afraid of what will happen to them if they do it 威慑力量；威慑因素；遏制物

e. g. The tough new law should act as a deterrent.

21. **unpunctuality** /ˌʌnpʌŋktʃuˈæləti/

n. the state of not being on time 不守时

22. **nauseous** /ˈnɔːziəs/

adj. making one want to vomit 想呕吐的；恶心的

e. g. A nauseous wave of pain broke over her.

23. **motive** /ˈməʊtɪv/

n. reason for doing something (行动的) 动机；缘由

e. g. The motives and objectives of British foreign policy are not known at present.

24. **repentance** /rɪˈpentəns/

n. the state of being sorry for doing something 后悔；悔改；悔意；忏悔

e. g. They showed no repentance during their trial.

25. **pernicious** /pəˈnɪʃəs/

adj. very harmful 有害的；恶性的

e. g. I did what I could, but her mother's influence was pernicious.

26. **irritability** /ˌɪrɪtəˈbɪləti/

n. the quality of being easily annoyed 易怒；急躁

27. **withhold** /wɪðˈhəʊld/

v. not let someone have something 拒绝给予；扣留

e. g. Financial aid for Britain has been withheld.

28. **remedy** /ˈremədi/

n. a successful way of dealing with a problem (问题的) 解决方法；解决良方

e. g. The remedy lies in the hands of the students themselves.

29. **retributive** /rɪˈtrɪbjətɪv/

adj. of or relating to or having the nature of retribution 惩罚性的

30. **remedial** /rɪˈmiːdiəl/

adj. intending to correct something that has been done wrong or that has not been successful 补救的；纠正的

e. g. Some authorities are now having to take remedial action.

31. **fixture** /ˈfɪkstʃə(r)/

n. the act of putting something in working order again 修复

32. **contented** /kənˈtentɪd/

adj. satisfied with life or situation 满足的；满意的

e. g. She was gazing at him with a soft, contented smile on her face.

33. **mal-adjusted** /ˌmæl əˈdʒʌstɪd/

adj. not well-adapted 适应不良的

34. **repulsion** /rɪˈpʌlʃn/

n. strong feeling of disgust 厌恶；憎恶；反感

e. g. She gave a dramatic shudder of repulsion.

35. **prudent** /ˈpruːdnt/

adj. sensible and careful 审慎的；慎重的；精明的

e. g. Being a prudent and cautious person, you realise that the problem must be resolved.

36. **barbarous** /ˈbɑːbərəs/

adj. rough and uncivilized 粗野的；未开化的；野蛮的

37. **superstition** /ˌsuːpəˈstɪʃn/

n. a belief in things that are not real or possible, for example magic 迷信；迷信观念

38. **brood** /bruːd/

v. hang over, as of something threatening, dark, or menacing; think about a lot, seriously and often unhappily 使人担忧；沉思；苦思冥想

e. g. The terrible vision brooded over her all day long.
   She constantly broods about her family.

39. **rarity** /ˈreərəti/

n. the quality of being very uncommon 稀有；罕见

e. g. This indicates the rarity of such attacks.

40. **mal-adjustment** /ˌmæl əˈdʒʌstmənt/

n. bad adjustment 适应不良

e. g. His son's mal-adjustment in school worries him.

41. **tenor** /ˈtenə/

n. the general meaning or mood 大意；主旨；要领

e. g. The whole tenor of discussions has changed.

42. **cramp** /kræmp/

v. restrict in some way 束缚；限制

e. g. Tighter trade restrictions might cramp economic growth.

43. **stifle** /ˈstaɪfl/

v. prevent something from continuing 扼杀；压制；抑止

44. **vigorously** /ˈvɪɡərəsli/

adv. involving using a lot of energy, usually to do short and repeated actions 剧烈地；强劲地

>>> Unit 9 Punishments and Rewards

e. g. Plants that are growing vigorously are less likely to be vulnerable to disease.

45. conventional /kənˈvenʃənl/

adj. that has been in use for a long time 通常的；传统的

e. g. These discs hold more than 400 times as much information as a conventional computer floppy disk.

46. canon /ˈkænən/

n. a general rule or principle 规范；规则；原则

e. g. The canons of good society are the same as the canons of art. Such was Dorian Gray's opinion.

47. abiding /əˈbaɪdɪŋ/

adj. having for a very long time(情感、记忆、兴趣等)持久的；长久的

e. g. He has a genuine and abiding love of the craft.

48. submit /səbˈmɪt/

v. formally send something to someone so that they can consider it or decide about it 提交；递呈

e. g. Head teachers yesterday submitted a claim for a 9 per cent pay rise.

49. purge /pɜːdʒ/

v. make yourself/somebody/something pure, healthy or clean by getting rid of bad thoughts or feelings 净化(心灵、风气等)；涤荡(污秽)

e. g. He closed his eyes and lay still, trying to purge his mind of anxiety.

Exercises for Text 1

I. Read the text and answer the questions.

1. What is the difference between discipline and order?
2. What is the psychological sequence of the disciplinary process?
3. How should teachers punish students so as to utterly help them?
4. What is the most important principle when teachers punish their students?
5. What are the implications of Percy Nunn's view for today's education?

II. Complete the sentences with the words below. Change the form where necessary.

brood	abiding	tenor	cramp	vigorously
prudent	rarity	nauseous	withhold	submit
purge	repulsion	deterrent	pernicious	retributive
conventional	contented	repress	motive	cannon

159

1. Those kids have been _____ for decades by the headmaster, so they want to leave this school.
2. They seriously believe that capital punishment is a(n) _____ so that it will stop lots of crimes.
3. If the patient is poorly nourished, the drugs make them feel _____. They might vomit.
4. The police have ruled out robbery as a(n) _____ for the killing, because the victim had lost nothing valuable.
5. There is a(n) _____ culture of excellence: everything has to be not merely good but the best. It has greatly harmed people's health.
6. The police _____ the witness's name yesterday in order to protect him.
7. Whenever he returns to this place, he is happy and _____. He is full of joy and satisfaction.
8. She gave a dramatic shudder of _____ when she saw the scene of murder.
9. It might be more _____ to get a second opinion before going ahead.
10. I guess everyone _____ over things once in a while when they are in agony.
11. It was a real prize due to its _____ and good condition.
12. Her dreams were troubled, reflecting the _____ of her waking hours.
13. In the Middle Ages, science was _____ by ignorance and superstition and couldn't develop very quickly.
14. The police _____ denied that excessive force had been used.
15. She's very _____ in her views and will not embrace new ideas.
16. The very first _____ of nursing is to keep the air inside as fresh as the air outside.
17. One of my _____ memories of him is of his wonderful singing to a small private party. I will never forget this.
18. They _____ their reports to the Chancellor yesterday.
19. Nothing could _____ the guilt from her mind and thus she had been brooding over her wrongdoings for a long time.
20. The essence of religion is life transmigration, _____ justice and undying of soul.

III. Translate the sentences into Chinese.

1. Though parts of our nature may resist this control, its acceptance must, on the whole, be willing acceptance—the spontaneous movement of a nature in which there is an inborn impulse towards greater perfection or "expressiveness".
2. First, there must be something that one genuinely desires to do, and one must be conscious either of one's inability or of someone else's superior ability to do it.

3. We can hardly leave the subject of discipline without some reference to the place of punishment in the school economy.
4. Disorderly and other mildly anti-social acts are often best punished by mere exclusion of the offender from the common occupation.
5. That mere repression is no cure, and that the true remedy lies in the "sublimation" of the criminal's misdirected energies.

READING & CRITICAL THINKING

Text 2
Corporal Punishments and Rewards

John Locke

1. **Punishments**—This being laid down in general, as the course ought to be taken, it's fit we now come to consider the parts of the discipline to be used, a little more particularly. I have spoken so much of carrying a strict hand over children, that perhaps I shall be suspected of not considering enough, what is due to their tender age and **constitutions**[1]. But that opinion will **vanish**[2], when you have heard me a little farther. For I am very apt to think, that great severity of punishment does but very little good; nay, great harm in education, and I believe it will be found, that those children who have been most **chastised**[3], seldom make the best men. All that I have **hitherto**[4] **contended**[5] for, is, that whatsoever **rigour**[6] is necessary, it is more to be used the younger children are; and having by a due application **wrought**[7] its effect, it is to be relaxed, and changed into a milder sort of government.

2. **Beating**—The usual lazy and short way by **chastisement**[8], and the **rod**[9], which is the only instrument of government that tutors generally know, or ever think of, is the most unfit of any to be used in education …

3. This kind of punishment **contributes**[10] not at all to the mastery of our natural **propensity**[11] to indulge corporal and present pleasure, and to avoid pain at any rate, but rather encourages it; and so strengthens that in us, which is the root of all vicious and wrong actions. For what motives, I pray, does a child act by, but of such pleasure and pain, that **drudges**[12] at his book against his **inclination**[13], or **abstains from**[14] eating **unwholesome**[15] fruit, that he takes pleasure in, only out of fear of whipping? He in this only prefers the greater corporal pleasure, or avoids the greater corporal pain; and what is it, to govern his actions, and direct his conduct, by such motives as these? What is it, I say, but to cherish that principle in him, which it is our business to root out and destroy? And therefore, I cannot think any correction

useful to a child, where the shame of suffering for having done **amiss**[16] does not work more upon him than the pain.

4. This sort of correction naturally breeds an **aversion**[17] to that which it is the tutor's business to create a liking to. How obvious is it to observe, that children come to hate things liked at first, as soon as they come to be whipped, or chid, and teased about them? And it is not to be wondered at in them, when grown men would not be able to be reconciled to anything by such ways. Who is there that would not be disgusted with any innocent recreation in itself indifferent to him, if he should with blows, or ill language, be haled to it, when he had no mind? Or be constantly so treated, for some circumstance in his application to it? This is natural to be so. Offensive circumstances ordinarily infect innocent things which they are joined with, and the very sight of a cup, wherein any one uses to take nauseous physic, turns his stomach, so that nothing will relish well out of it, though the cup be never so clean and well-shaped, and of the richest materials.

5. Such a sort of slavish discipline makes a slavish temper. The child submits, and dissembles obedience, whilst the fear of the rod hangs over him; but when that is removed, and, by being out of sight, he can promise himself **impunity**[18], he gives the greater **scope**[19] to his natural inclination, which by this way is not at all altered, but on the contrary heightened and increased in him, and after such **restraint**[20], breaks out usually with the more violence. Or, if severity carried to the highest pitch does prevail, and works a cure upon the present **unruly**[21] distemper, it is often bringing in the room of it a worse and more dangerous disease, by breaking the mind; and then, in the place of a disorderly young fellow, you have a low-spirited, **moped**[22] creature: who, however with his unnatural **sobriety**[23] he may please silly people, who commend tame, unactive children because they make no noise, nor give them any trouble; yet, at last, will probably prove as uncomfortable a thing to his friends, as he will be, all his life, an useless thing to himself and others.

6. **Rewards**—Beating then, and all other sorts of slavish and corporal punishments, are not the discipline fit to be used in the education of those we would have wise, good, and ingenuous men; and therefore, very rarely to be applied, and that only in great occasions, and cases of extremity. On the other side, to flatter children by rewards of things that are pleasant to them, is as carefully to be avoided. He that will give to his son apples, or sugar-plums,

or what else of this kind he is most delighted with, to make him learn his book, does but **authorize**[24] his love of pleasure, and cocker up that dangerous propensity, which he ought by all means to subdue and stifle in him. You can never hope to teach him to master it whilst you compound for the check you give his inclination in one place, by the satisfaction you propose to it in another. To make a good, wise and virtuous man, it is fit he should learn to cross his appetite, and deny his inclination to riches, finery, or pleasing his palate, etc., whenever his reason advises the contrary, and his duty requires it. But when you draw him to do anything that is fit, by the offer of money, or reward the pains of learning his book, by the pleasure of a **luscious**[25] morsel; when you promise him a lace-**cravat**[26], or a fine new suit, upon performance of some of his little tasks; what do you, by proposing these as rewards, but allow them to be the good things he should aim at, and thereby encourage his longing for them, and accustom him to place his happiness in them? Thus people, to prevail with children to be **industrious**[27] about their grammar, dancing, or some other such matter of no great moment to the happiness or usefulness of their lives, by misapplied rewards and punishments, sacrifice their virtue, invert the order of their education, and teach them luxury, pride, of **covetousness**[28], etc. For in this way, flattering those wrong inclinations, which they should restrain and suppress, they lay the foundations of those future vices, which cannot be avoided, but by curbing our desires, and accustoming them early to submit to reason.

7. I say not this, that I would have children kept from the conveniences or pleasures of life, that are not **injurious**[29] to their health or virtue. On the contrary, I would have their lives made as pleasant, and as agreeable to them as may be, in a plentiful enjoyment of whatsoever might innocently delight them: provided it be with this caution, that they have those enjoyments only as the consequences of the state of **esteem**[30] and acceptation they are in with their parents and governors; but they should never be offered or bestowed on them, as the reward of this or that particular performance, that they show an aversion to, or to which they would not have applied themselves without that temptation. But if you take away the rod on one hand, and these little encouragements, which they are taken with, on the other, how then (will you say) shall children be governed? Remove hope and fear, and there is an end of all discipline. I grant, that good and evil, reward and punishment, are the

>>> Unit 9　Punishments and Rewards

only motives to a rational creature; these are the spur and reins whereby all mankind are set on work and guided, and therefore they are to be made use of to children too. For I advise their parents and governors always to carry this in their minds, that they are to be treated as rational creatures.

8. Rewards, I grant, and punishments must be proposed to children, if we intend to work upon them. The mistake, I imagine, is that those that are generally made use of are ill chosen. The pains and pleasures of the body are, I think, of ill consequence, when made the rewards and punishments, whereby men would prevail on their children: for they serve but to increase and strengthen those appetites which it's our business to subdue and master. What principle of virtue do you lay in a child, if you will **redeem**[31] his desires of one pleasure by the proposal of another? This is but to enlarge his appetite, and instruct it to wander. If a child cries for an unwholesome and dangerous fruit, you purchase his quiet by giving him a less hurtful sweetmeat; this perhaps may preserve his health, but spoils his mind, and sets that farther out of order. For here you only change the object, but flatter still his appetite, and allow that must be satisfied, wherein, as I have showed, lies the root of the mischief, and till you bring him to be able to bear a denial of that satisfaction, the child may at present be quiet and orderly, but the disease is not cured. By this way of proceeding, you **foment**[32] and cherish in him, that which is the spring from whence all the evil flows, which will be sure on the next occasion to break out again with more violence, give him stronger longings, and you more trouble.

(From John Locke's *Some Thoughts Concerning Education*)

Vocabulary

1. **constitution** /ˌkɒnstɪˈtjuːʃn/
   n. the way in which someone or something is composed 体格
   e.g. He must have an extremely strong constitution.
2. **vanish** /ˈvænɪʃ/
   v. cease to exist 消失
3. **chastise** /tʃæˈstaɪz/
   v. punish severely 严惩

e. g. He chastised the team for their lack of commitment.

4. **hitherto** /ˌhɪðəˈtuː/

adv. until the present time 迄今为止

e. g. The polytechnics have hitherto been at an unfair disadvantage in competing for pupils and money.

5. **contend** /kənˈtend/

v. maintain or assert 声称；主张

6. **rigour** /ˈrɪɡə(r)/

n. excessive sternness 严酷；严厉

e. g. This crime must be treated with the full rigour of the law.

7. **wrought** /rɔːt/

v. the past tense and past participle of "work" 造成

8. **chastisement** /tʃæˈstaɪzmənt/

n. punishment 惩罚

9. **rod** /rɒd/

n. a long straight piece of wood, metal or glass 棍棒

10. **contribute to**

lead to 导致

e. g. Honesty and hard work contribute to success and happiness.

11. **propensity** /prəˈpensəti/

n. an inclination to do something 倾向；习性

e. g. She has a propensity to exaggerate.

12. **drudge** /drʌdʒ/

v. work hard 做苦工

13. **inclination** /ˌɪnklɪˈneɪʃn/

n. a feeling that makes you want to do something 倾向

e. g. You must follow your own inclinations when choosing a career.

14. **abstain from**

refrain from 戒除；不参加

e. g. Athletes usually abstain from smoking.

15. **unwholesome** /ˌʌnˈhəʊlsəm/

adj. harmful to physical or moral well-being 不卫生的

e. g. Unwholesome diet will hurt our health.

16. **amiss** /əˈmɪs/

adv. in an improper, mistaken or unfortunate manner 有毛病地；恰当地

adj. in an improper, mistaken or unfortunate manner 出了岔子的；不恰当的

e. g. If you think him guilty, you judge amiss.

A bit of charm and humour would not go amiss.

17. aversion /əˈvɜːʃn/

n. a feeling of intense dislike 厌恶；反感

e. g. He had an aversion to getting up early.

18. impunity /ɪmˈpjuːnəti/

n. exemption from punishment or loss 不受惩罚；无罪

e. g. If laws are not enforced, crimes are committed with impunity.

19. scope /skəʊp/

n. the opportunity or ability to do or achieve something（活动或能力的）余地

e. g. There's still plenty of scope for improvement.

20. restraint /rɪˈstreɪnt/

n. a rule or condition that limits freedom 抑制

e. g. The teacher was praised for his restraint in handling the chaos.

21. unruly /ʌnˈruːli/

adj. noisy and lacking in restraint or discipline 不守规矩的；任性的；难驾驭的；难控制的

e. g. He is an unruly boy and nobody can control him.

22. mope /məʊp/

v. behave in a way that shows you are unhappy and depressed 闷闷不乐；自怨自艾

23. sobriety /səˈbraɪəti/

n. the state of being sober 清醒

24. authorize /ˈɔːθəraɪz/

v. give official permission for something, or for somebody to do something;（archaic）justify 认可；允许

e. g. The students were authorized to search for the information they needed in the big library.

25. luscious /ˈlʌʃəs/

adj. extremely pleasing to the sense of taste 美味的；过分甜美的；腻人的

e. g. They do not like the luscious cake.

26. cravat /krəˈvæt/

n. neckwear worn in a slipknot with long ends overlapping vertically in front（系在衬衫衣领里面的）男式围巾

27. industrious /ɪnˈdʌstriəs/

adj. characterized by hard work and perseverance 勤劳的；勤奋的

e. g. She was an industrious and willing worker.

28. covetousness /ˈkʌvətəsnɪs/

n. an envious eagerness to possess something 贪婪；贪心

e. g. Covetousness is the root of all evil.

29. injurious /ɪnˈdʒʊəriəs/

adj. harmful to living things 有害的；伤害的

e.g. Reading while riding in a car is injurious to one's eyes.

30. esteem /ɪˈstiːm/

n. a feeling of admiration and respect for someone 尊重；敬重

e.g. She is held in high esteem.

31. redeem /rɪˈdiːm/

v. save from sins 赎回

e.g. Olivier's performance redeemed an otherwise second-rate play.

32. foment /fəʊˈment/

v. cause something to develop 煽动；助长

Exercises for Text 2

I. Decide whether the statements are true (T) or false (F) according to the text.

1. Severe punishment does a lot of good to children.
2. Children who are most often punished will grow into the best men.
3. Punishment encourages our nature to indulge present pleasure and avoid pain. It is the root of vicious and wrong actions.
4. The shame about doing something wrong works better than the pain following the punishment.
5. Rewarding children with things that are pleasant to them needs to be avoided.

II. Translate the following sentences with the key words in the parentheses.

1. 这些植物经受不住严冬的考验。(rigour)
2. 他表现出暴力的倾向，这让人害怕。(propensity)
3. 他一开始就表现出不听命令的倾向。(inclination)
4. 昨天旷工的工人被暂时停职。(abstain)
5. 很多人生来讨厌昆虫。(aversion)
6. 有了这笔额外的资金，我们就能对设备加以改进。(scope)
7. 这个班的学生不守规矩的行为使老师感到羞愧。(unruly)
8. 我已授权他在我外出时代理我的职务。(authorize)
9. 勤奋的学生通常有好成绩。(industrious)
10. 他的行为有损于大多数人的利益。(injurious)

III. Explain the following sentences in your own words.

1. I have spoken so much of carrying a strict hand over children, that perhaps I shall be suspected of not considering enough, what is due to their tender age and constitutions.

2. He in this only prefers the greater corporal pleasure, or avoids the greater corporal pain; and what is it, to govern his actions, and direct his conduct, by such motives as these?
3. And the very sight of a cup, wherein any one uses to take nauseous physic, turns his stomach, so that nothing will relish well out of it, though the cup be never so clean and well-shaped, and of the richest materials.
4. Yet, at last, will probably prove as uncomfortable a thing to his friends, as he will be, all his life, a useless thing to himself and others.
5. What do you, by proposing these as rewards, but allow them to be the good things he should aim at, and thereby encourage his longing for them, and accustom him to place his happiness in them?

Learning Strategies

Scanning

Scanning means moving our eyes quickly over the text to look for specific information. We do not need to read every word. Instead, we look for the key information that will answer our questions.

For example, to know the difference between discipline and order, we can read the first paragraph of Text 1 very quickly to get the answer.

Now, you can read the third and fourth paragraph of Text 1 and find out the most important principles of punishment.

Unit Project

Work in groups to make research about articles about the principle of punishment and write a report of 800 words.
1. Interview some students about how they are punished when they do something wrong and what they think of those ways of punishment.
2. Find articles related to the principle of punishment.
3. Hold a discussion in groups about whether you agree with the views of those articles.
4. Give an analysis of those articles by referring to the two authors' view.

Unit 10

The Way to Promote Retention

Pre-reading questions:

1. What do you know about David Ausubel's view on the role of subsumption in the retention of information?
2. What do you know about J. S. Bruner's view on the importance of structure in the retention of information?

>>> Unit 10　The Way to Promote Retention

READING & CRITICAL THINKING

Text 1

Meaningful Learning

David Ausubel

1. Plausible reasons exist for believing that **rotely**[1] and meaningfully learned materials are organized much differently in consciousness and hence conform to quite different principles of learning and forgetting. First, meaningfully learned materials have been related to existing concepts in cognitive structure in ways making possible the understanding of various kinds of significant (e.g., derivative, descriptive, supportive) relationships. Most new **ideational**[2] materials that pupils encounter in a school setting are relatable to a previously learned background of meaningful ideas and information. In fact, the curriculum is **deliberately**[3] organized in this fashion to provide for the untraumatic introduction of new facts and concepts. Rotely learned materials, on the other hand, are discrete and isolated entities which have not been related to established concepts in the learner's cognitive structure. (Depending on their logical relatability to a particular learner's cognitive structure, they may or may not be potentially meaningful to begin with.) Second, because they are not anchored to existing ideational systems, rotely learned materials (unless greatly overlearned or endowed with unusual vividness) are much more vulnerable to forgetting, i.e., have a much shorter **retention**[4] span.

2. The above differences between rote and meaningful learning categories have important implications for the underlying kinds of learning and retention processes involved in each category. Rotely learned materials are essentially isolated from cognitive structure, and hence are primarily influenced by the interfering effects of similar rote materials learned immediately before or after the learning task. Thus, it is not unreasonable to explain the learning and retention of discrete rote units in such stimulus-response terms as intra- and inter-task similarity, response competition, and stimulus or response

generalization. The learning and retention of meaningful materials, however, are primarily influenced by the **attributes**[5] of relevant subsuming concepts in cognitive structure with which they interact. Compared to this extended interaction with established ideational components, **concurrent**[6] interfering effects have relatively little influence and explanatory value.

The Subsumption Process in Learning and Forgetting

3. The model of cognitive organization proposed for the learning and retention of meaningful materials assumes the existence of a cognitive structure that is **hierarchically**[7] organized in terms of highly inclusive conceptual traces under which are subsumed traces of less inclusive sub-concepts as well as traces of specific informational data. The major organizational principle, in other words, is that of progressive differentiation of trace systems of a given sphere of knowledge from regions of greater to lesser inclusiveness, each linked to the next higher step in the hierarchy through a process of subsumption. It is incorrect, however, to conceive of this mode of organization as deductive in nature. The inductive-deductive issue is only relevant in considering the method of acquiring or presenting generalizations and supportive data, and the sequential procedure adopted in problem-solving. Irrespective of how they are acquired in the first place (inductively or deductively), new materials are incorporated into total cognitive organization in accordance with the same principle of progressive differentiation.

4. Thus, as new material enters the cognitive field, it interacts with and is appropriately subsumed under a relevant and more inclusive conceptual system. The very fact that it is **subsumable**[8] (relatable to stable elements in cognitive structure) accounts for its meaningfulness and makes possible the perception of **insightful**[9] relationships. If it were not subsumable, it would constitute rote material and form discrete and isolated traces.

5. The initial effects of subsumption, therefore, may be described as **facilitation**[10] of both learning and retention. Only **orienting**[11], relational, and **cataloguing**[12] operations are involved at first. These **preliminary**[13] operations are obviously essential for meaningful learning and retention, since the incorporation of new material into existing cognitive structure necessarily presupposes consistency with the **prevailing**[14] principle of organization. Furthermore, subsumption of the traces of the learning task by an established

ideational system provides anchorage for the new material, and thus constitutes the most orderly, efficient and stable way of retaining it for future availability. Hence, for a variable period of time, the recently catalogued sub-concepts and informational data can be dissociated from their subsuming concepts and are reproducible as individually identifiable entities.

6. Although the stability of meaningful material is initially **enhanced**[15] by anchorage to relevant conceptual **foci**[16] in the learner's cognitive structure, such material is gradually subjected to the **erosive**[17] influence of the conceptualizing trend in cognitive organization. Because it is more **economical**[18] and less burdensome to retain a single inclusive concept than to remember a large number of more specific items, the import of the latter tends to be incorporated by the generalized meaning of the former. When this second or **obliterative**[19] stage of subsumption begins, the specific items become progressively less dissociable as entities in their own right until they are no longer available and are said to be forgotten.

7. This process of memorial reduction to the least **common denominator**[20] capable of representing cumulative prior experience is very similar to the reduction process characterizing concept formation. A single abstract concept is more **manipulable**[21] for cognitive purposes than the dozen diverse instances from which its commonality is **abstracted**[22]; and similarly, the memorial **residue**[23] of ideational experience is also more functional for future learning and problem-solving occasions when stripped of its **tangential**[24] modifiers, particularized **connotations**[25], and less clear and **discriminable**[26] **implications**[27]. Hence, barring repetition or some other special reason [e. g., primacy, uniqueness, enhanced discriminability, or the availability of a specially relevant and stable subsumer (see below)] for the **perpetuation**[28] of dissociability, specific items of meaningful experience that are supportive of or **correlative**[29] to an established conceptual entity tend gradually to undergo obliterative subsumption.

Learning versus Forgetting

8. In reception (as contrasted to discovery) learning, the distinctive attribute of both learning and forgetting is a change in the availability or future reproducibility of the learning material. Learning represents an **increment**[30] in availability (i. e., the situation prevailing after initial exposure to or repetition of the material), whereas forgetting represents a **decrement**[31] in availability

(i.e., the situation prevailing after a single exposure of between two exposures of the material). Retention, therefore, is largely a later **temporal**[32] phase and **diminished**[33] aspect of the same phenomenon or functional capacity (the availability of **internalized**[34] material) involved in learning itself. Later availability is obviously a function of initial availability. In the absence of intervening practice, therefore, delayed retention cannot possibly **surpass**[35] immediate retention. The common phenomenon of **reminiscence**[36] reflects either the operation of a drive state temporarily lowering thresholds of availability at a later testing of retention, or the subsequent release (disinhibition) of **transitory**[37] **inhibitory**[38] conditions (e.g., **repression**[39]; initial confusion after presentation of new material) operative immediately after learning.

9. The relationship between meaningful learning and forgetting is even closer than that already indicated for reception learning generally. Meaningful retention is not only a later **attenuated**[40] manifestation of the same availability function established during learning, but is also a later temporal phase of the same interactional process underlying this availability. During the learning phase, new ideational material forms an interactional product with a subsuming focus in cognitive structure, and depending on various factors (see below), has a given degree of dissociability **therefrom**[41]. Continued interaction results in a gradual decrease in the dissociability of the new material (i.e., in forgetting) until the interactional product is reduced to a least common denominator capable of representing the entire complex, namely, to the subsuming concept itself. The same cognitive factors determining the original degree of dissociability at the time of learning (initial interaction) also determine the rate at which dissociability is subsequently lost during retention (later interaction). In rote learning, on the other hand, cognitive interaction, by definition, does not take place. Hence, rote learning represents an increment in availability involving one discrete cognitive process and set of variables, and rote forgetting represents a loss in this availability due to interference from another discrete process (and group of variables) set in motion shortly before or after learning.

(From David Ausubel's "A Subsumption Theory of Meaningful Verbal Learning and Retention")

Vocabulary

1. rotely /ˈrəʊtli/

adv. memorizing by repetition 死记硬背地

2. ideational /ˌaɪdɪˈeɪʃənəl/

adj. being (or being of the nature of) a notion or concept 概念的

3. deliberately /dɪˈlɪbərətli/

adv. with intention; in an intentional manner 有意地

e. g. She's been deliberately ignoring him all day.

4. retention /rɪˈtenʃn/

n. the power of retaining and recalling past experience 记忆；保持；维持

e. g. Research indicates that humor can increase retention from 15% to 50%.

5. attribute /əˈtrɪbjuːt/

n. a construct whereby objects or individuals can be distinguished 性质

e. g. What attributes should a good manager possess?

6. concurrent /kənˈkʌrənt/

adj. occurring or operating at the same time 同时发生的

e. g. The exhibition reflected concurrent developments abroad.

7. hierarchically /ˌhaɪəˈrɑːkɪkli/

adv. being classified according to various criteria into successive levels or layers 分等级地

8. subsumable /səbˈsjuːməbl/

adj. that can be included 可归入的

9. insightful /ˈɪnsaɪtfʊl/

adj. exhibiting insight or clear and deep perception 富有洞察力的

e. g. At that moment the world lost one of its most talented and insightful poets.

10. facilitation /fəˌsɪlɪˈteɪʃn/

n. the process of making something easier 促进；便利

11. orient /ˈɔːrient/

v. determine one's position with reference to another point （使）朝向；面向

e. g. A lot of training is orientated around communications skills.

12. catalogue /ˈkætəlɒɡ/

v. make a catalog of 列入目录

e. g. The Royal Greenwich Observatory was founded to observe and catalogue the stars.

13. preliminary /prɪˈlɪmɪnəri/

adj. designed to orient or acquaint with a situation before proceeding 初步的；预备的

e. g. The preliminary market test is about to begin next week.

14. prevail /prɪˈveɪl/

v. be larger in number, quantity, power, status or importance 流行；盛行

e. g. We were horrified at the conditions prevailing in local prisons.

15. enhance /ɪnˈhɑːns/

v. make better or more attractive 提高；增强

e. g. Good lighting will enhance any room.

16. foci /ˈfəʊsaɪ/

n. plural form of focus

17. erosive /ɪˈrəʊsɪv/

adj. wearing away by friction 腐蚀性的；侵蚀性的

e. g. Bleeding from erosive gastritis was rarely life-threatening.

18. economical /ˌiːkəˈnɒmɪkl/

adj. avoiding waste 节约的

e. g. A small car is more economical to run.

19. obliterative /əˈblɪtəreɪtɪv/

adj. tending to make inconspicuous 被遮蔽的

20. common denominator /ˈkɒmən dɪˈnɒmɪneɪtə(r)/

a number which can be divided exactly by all the denominators in a group of fractions; a characteristic or attitude that is shared by all members of a group of people 公分母；共同之处

21. manipulable /məˈnɪpjuləbl/

adj. that can be controlled 可操纵的

22. abstract /æbˈstrækt/

v. give an abstract (of) 提炼

e. g. She abstracted the main points from the argument.

23. residue /ˈrezɪdjuː/

n. matter that remains after something has been removed 残余

e. g. Always using the same shampoo means that a residue can build up on the hair.

24. tangential /tænˈdʒenʃl/

adj. of superficial relevance if any 间接相关的；外围的

e. g. Too much time was spent discussing tangential issues.

25. connotation /ˌkɒnəˈteɪʃn/

n. an idea that is implied or suggested 内涵；含义

e. g. The word "professional" has connotations of skill and excellence.

26. discriminable /dɪsˈkrɪmɪnəbl/

adj. that can be distinguished 可分辨的；可辨别的

27. implication /ˌɪmplɪˈkeɪʃn/

n. something that is inferred 含义;蕴含

e. g. The implication in his article is that being a housewife is greatly inferior to every other occupation.

28. perpetuation /pəˌpetʃuˈeɪʃn/

n. the act of prolonging something 永存;不朽

29. correlative /kəˈrelətɪv/

adj. mutually related 相关的

e. g. The correlative data also indicates that the production of distilling liquor started before the Yuan Dynasty.

30. increment /ˈɪŋkrəmənt/

n. a process of becoming larger or longer or more numerous or more important 增长

e. g. Each increment of knowledge tells us more of our world.

31. decrement /ˈdekrɪmənt/

n. a process of becoming smaller or shorter 减量;缩减

32. temporal /ˈtempərəl/

adj. of or relating to or limited by time 时间的

e. g. One is also able to see how specific acts are related to a temporal and spatial context.

33. diminish /dɪˈmɪnɪʃ/

v. decrease in size, extent, or range 减少;消弱

e. g. That's not to diminish the importance of his discoveries.

34. internalize /ɪnˈtɜːnəlaɪz/

v. incorporate within oneself; make subjective or personal 使内在化

e. g. Over time she internalized her parents' attitudes.

35. surpass /səˈpɑːs/

v. be or do something to a greater degree 超过

e. g. The number of multiple births has surpassed 100,000 for the first time.

36. reminiscence /ˌremɪˈnɪsns/

n. the process of remembering (especially the process of recovering information by mental effort) 回忆

e. g. The book is a collection of his reminiscences about the actress.

37. transitory /ˈtrænzətri/

adj. enduring a very short time 不持续的;短暂的

e. g. Most teenage romances are transitory.

38. inhibitory /ɪnˈhɪbɪtəri/

adj. restrictive of action 禁止的;抑制的

39. repression /rɪˈpreʃn/

n. the act of repressing; control by holding down 压抑

40. attenuate /əˈtenjueɪt/

v. weaken the consistency of 减弱；变小

e.g. The drug attenuates the effects of the virus.

41. therefrom /ˌðeəˈfrɒm/

adv. from that place or from there 从那里

Exercises for Text 1

I. Read the text and answer the questions.

1. What is the difference between meaningful learning and rote learning?
2. What is the organizing principle of the cognitive structure for meaningful learning?
3. How does subsumption work in the process of learning?
4. What is the distinctive attribute of both learning and forgetting in reception learning?
5. What are the implications of subsumption theory for modern education?

II. Complete the sentences with the words below. Change the form where necessary.

prevail	plausible	enhance	economical	transitory
retention	concurrent	erosive	implication	attenuate
attribute	orient	correlative	surpass	cumulative
insightful	preliminary	diminish	reminiscence	deliberately

1. I believe he didn't do this on purpose. The possible _____ explanation is that he was misled by someone.
2. I have a real problem with _____ of information. I always forget what I try to remember.
3. Patience is one of the most important _____ in a teacher.
4. Galerie St. Etienne is holding three _____ exhibitions, so you need to choose among the three.
5. She offered some really interesting, _____ observations, which will give you lots of inspirations.
6. The university is strongly _____ towards research. Teaching is not its priority.
7. In this paper, we will just give a(n) _____ explanation. We will give a more elaborate explanation in the next paper.
8. Those beliefs still _____ among certain social groups and greatly influence their thinking.

9. This is an opportunity to _____ the reputation of the company.
10. By the _____ processes, the glacier is reduced.
11. It was more _____ to buy the bigger size, so we chose to buy the bigger one in order to save money.
12. The development of the site will have _____ for the surrounding countryside and promote its development.
13. The teachers' motives and their actual degree of participation are highly _____. The stronger their motives are, the more active their participation is.
14. Don't let him _____ your achievements. You should find a better cooperator who will readily recognize what you have achieved.
15. Her cooking was always good, but this time she had _____ herself. It indicated that she had never stopped improving herself.
16. Her music is full of _____ of African rhythms and this makes the listeners begin to miss the African music.
17. Once again, Vermeer succeeded in transforming a(n) _____ image into one of eternal truth.
18. Theirs had been an increasingly _____ relationship. At last, they looked like strangers to each other.
19. She was accused of _____ misleading her colleagues although she claimed that she didn't know the truth herself.
20. The benefits from eating fish are _____. Gradually we will see the benefits.

III. Translate the sentences into Chinese.

1. First, meaningfully learned materials have been related to existing concepts in cognitive structure in ways making possible the understanding of various kinds of significant relationships.
2. Because they are not anchored to existing ideational systems, rotely learned materials (unless greatly overlearned or endowed with unusual vividness) are much more vulnerable to forgetting, i.e., have a much shorter retention span.
3. The learning and retention of meaningful materials, however, are primarily influenced by the attributes of relevant subsuming concepts in cognitive structure with which they interact.
4. If it were not subsumable, it would constitute rote material and form discrete and isolated traces.
5. These preliminary operations are obviously essential for meaningful learning and retention, since the incorporation of new material into existing cognitive structure necessarily presupposes consistency with the prevailing principle of organization.

Text 2

The Process of Education

J. S. Bruner

1. The first object of any act of learning, over and beyond the pleasure it may give, is that it should serve us in the future. Learning should not only take us somewhere; it should allow us later to go further more easily. There are two ways in which learning serves the future. One is through its specific applicability to tasks that are highly similar to those we originally learned to perform. Psychologists refer to this phenomenon as specific transfer of training; perhaps it should be called the extension of habits or associations. Its utility appears to be limited in the main to what we usually speak of as skills. Having learned how to hammer nails, we are better able later to learn how to hammer tacks or chip wood. Learning in school undoubtedly creates skills of a kind that transfers to activities encountered later, either in school or after. A second way in which earlier learning renders later performance more efficient is through what is conveniently called nonspecific transfer or, more accurately, the transfer of principles and attitudes. In essence, it consists of learning initially not a skill but a general idea, which can then be used as a basis for recognizing **subsequent**[1] problems as special cases of the idea originally mastered. This type of transfer is at the heart of the educational process—the continual broadening and deepening of knowledge in terms of basic and general ideas.

2. The continuity of learning that is produced by the second type of transfer, transfer of principles, is dependent upon mastery of the structure of the subject matter, as structure was described in the preceding chapter. That is to say, in order for a person to be able to recognize the applicability or inapplicability of an idea to a new situation and to broaden his learning thereby, he must have clearly in mind the general nature of the phenomenon with which he is dealing. The more fundamental or basic is the idea he has

learned, almost by definition, the greater will be its breadth of applicability to new problems. Indeed, this is almost a **tautology**[2], for what is meant by "fundamental" in this sense is precisely that an idea has wide as well as powerful applicability. It is simple enough to proclaim, of course, that school **curricula**[3] and methods of teaching should be **geared**[4] to the teaching of fundamental ideas in whatever subject is being taught. But as soon as one makes such a statement, a host of problems arise, many of which can be solved only with the aid of considerably more research. We turn to some of these now.

3. The first and most obvious problem is how to construct curricula that can be taught by ordinary teachers to ordinary students and that at the same time reflect clearly the basic or underlying principles of various fields of inquiry. The problem is twofold: first, how to have the basic subjects rewritten and their teaching materials **revamped**[5] in such a way that the **pervading**[6] and powerful ideas and attitudes relating to them are given a central role; second, how to match the levels of these materials to the capacities of students of different abilities at different grades in school.

4. There is at least one major matter that is left unsettled even by a large-scale revision of curricula in the direction indicated. Mastery of the fundamental ideas of a field involves not only the grasping of general principles, but also the development of an attitude toward learning and inquiry, toward guessing and hunches, toward the possibility of solving problems on one's own. Just as a physicist has certain attitudes about the **ultimate**[7] orderliness of nature and a conviction that order can be discovered, so a young physics student needs some working version of these attitudes if he is to organize his learning in such a way as to make what he learns usable and meaningful in his thinking. To **instill**[8] such attitudes by teaching requires something more than the mere presentation of fundamental ideas. Just what it takes to bring off such teaching is something on which a great deal of research is needed, but it would seem that an important ingredient is a sense of excitement about discovery—discovery of regularities of **previously**[9] unrecognized relations and similarities between ideas, with a resulting sense of self-confidence in one's abilities. Various people who have worked on curricula in science and mathematics have urged that it is possible to present the fundamental structure of a discipline in such a way as to preserve some of the

exciting sequences that lead a student to discover for himself.

5. Inherent in the preceding discussions are at least four general claims that can be made for teaching the fundamental structure of a subject, claims in need of detailed study.

6. The first is that understanding fundamentals makes a subject more **comprehensible**[10]. This is true not only in physics and mathematics, where we have principally illustrated the point, but equally in the social studies and literature.

7. The second point relates to human memory. Perhaps the most basic thing that can be said about human memory, after a century of **intensive**[11] research, is that unless detail is placed into a structured pattern, it is rapidly forgotten. Detailed material is conserved in memory by the use of simplified ways of representing it. These simplified representations have what may be called a "**regenerative**"[12] character. A good example of this regenerative property of long-term memory can be found in science. A scientist does not try to remember the distances **traversed**[13] by falling bodies in different **gravitational**[14] fields over different periods of time. What he carries in memory instead is a **formula**[15] that permits him with varying degrees of accuracy to regenerate the details on which the more easily remembered formula is based. So, he commits to memory the formula $s = 1/2\ gf$ and not a handbook of distances, times, and gravitational constants.

8. Third, an understanding of fundamental principles and ideas, as noted earlier, appears to be the main road to adequate "transfer of training". To understand something as a specific instance of a more general case—which is what understanding a more fundamental principle or structure means—is to have learned not only a specific thing but also a model for understanding other things like it that one may encounter.

9. The fourth claim for emphasis on structure and principles in teaching is that by constantly reexamining material taught in elementary and secondary schools for its fundamental character, one is able to narrow the gap between "advanced" knowledge and "**elementary**"[16] knowledge. Part of the difficulty now found in the progression from primary school through high school to college is that material learned earlier is either out of date or misleading by virtue of its **lagging**[17] too far behind developments in a field. This gap can be reduced by the kind of emphasis set forth in the preceding discussion.

(From J. S. Bruner's *The Process of Education*)

>>> Unit 10 The Way to Promote Retention

Vocabulary

1. subsequent /ˈsʌbsɪkwənt/

adj. happening or existing after the time or event that has just been referred to 随后的；后来的

e. g. The increase of population in subsequent years was dramatic.

2. tautology /tɔːˈtɒlədʒi/

n. the use of different words to say the same thing twice in the same statement 同义反复；赘述

3. curricula /kəˈrɪkjələ/

n. pl of curriculum which means one particular course of study that is taught in a school, college, or university（特定的）课程

4. gear /gɪə(r)/

v. be organized or designed in order to achieve certain purpose 使为……而准备；使为了达到……而做好准备；使为……目的而设计

e. g. My training was geared towards winning gold in Munich.

5. revamp /ˌriːˈvæmp/

v. make changes to something in order to try and improve it 修补；修改；改进

6. pervade /pəˈveɪd/

v. become a noticeable feature throughout something 贯穿；弥漫；渗透

e. g. The smell of sawdust and glue pervaded the factory.

7. ultimate /ˈʌltɪmət/

adj. final 最后的；最终的

e. g. He said it was still not possible to predict the ultimate outcome.

8. instill /ɪnˈstɪl/

v. gradually impart 逐步灌输

e. g. They tried to instill such new ideas into students' minds.

9. previously /ˈpriːviəsli/

adv. at some time before 先前；以前

e. g. Guyana's railways were previously owned by private companies.

10. comprehensible /ˌkɒmprɪˈhensəbl/

adj. that can be understood 能懂的；可以理解的

e. g. He spoke abruptly, in barely comprehensible Arabic.

11. intensive /ɪnˈtensɪv/

adj. concentrating a lot of effort or people on one particular task in order to try to achieve a great deal in a short time 加强的；集中的；密集的

e. g. Several days and nights of intensive negotiations have made them very tired.

12. regenerative /rɪˈdʒenərətɪv/

adj. causing something to heal or become active again after it has been damaged or inactive 有再生作用的；有再造能力的

e. g. The regenerative power of nature is really amazing.

13. traverse /trəˈvɜːs, ˈtrævɜːs/

v. go across 横穿；横越；穿过

14. gravitational /ˌɡrævɪˈteɪʃnl/

adj. relating to or resulting from the force of gravity 与引力有关的；引力所致的

15. formula /ˈfɔːmjələ/

n. a group of letters, numbers, or other symbols which represents a scientific or mathematical rule 公式；方程式

16. elementary /ˌelɪˈmentri/

adj. very simple and basic 简单的；基本的

e. g. Elementary computer skills are necessary in getting a job.

17. lag /læɡ/

v. slower than that of the other 落后；赶不上

e. g. The restructuring of the pattern of consumption in Britain also lagged behind.

Exercises for Text 2

I. Decide whether the statements are true (T) or false (F) according to the text.

1. The first object of learning is that it is supposed to help us in the future.
2. We can make our learning serve the future by applying what we have learned in a similar task.
3. The transfer of principles and attitudes will not help our later performance.
4. In order to apply an idea to a new situation, we must know the general nature of the phenomena we will deal with.
5. Understanding fundamental structure can make us understand a subject better.

II. Translate the following sentences with the key words in the parentheses.

1. 随后发生的事使之前所关注的那些问题显得无足轻重。(subsequent)
2. 大学有时满足不了学生的需求。(gear)
3. 整所房子都充满了酸味。(pervade)
4. 最终目的是进一步拓展该网络。(ultimate)
5. 我认为给运动员灌输自豪感是很重要的。(instill)
6. 合同签给了一个之前并不知名的公司。(previously)
7. 这本书普通读者也能看得懂。(comprehensible)
8. 每个辅导员在上岗前都要接受强化培训。(intensive)

>>> Unit 10 The Way to Promote Retention

9. 我走过狭窄的人行天桥,来到那个大家熟知的商场。(traverse)
10. 我对这门学科的了解只是初级水平。(elementary)

III. Explain the following sentences in your own words.

1. Just what it takes to bring off such teaching is something on which a great deal of research is needed.
2. What we have learned in primary and secondary schools might be out of date or misleading.
3. Detailed material is conserved in memory by the use of simplified ways of representing it.
4. Perhaps the most basic thing that can be said about human memory, after a century of intensive research, is that unless detail is placed into a structured pattern, it is rapidly forgotten.
5. By constantly reexamining material taught in elementary and secondary schools for its fundamental character, one is able to narrow the gap between "advanced" knowledge and "elementary" knowledge.

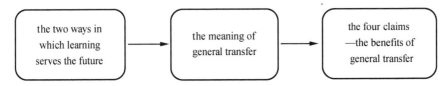

Understanding by Mind Map

When the idea of an article is complicated, we can use mind map to help us understand the structure of the article.

For example, to understand Bruner's idea in the second article, we can draw the following map:

the two ways in which learning serves the future → the meaning of general transfer → the four claims —the benefits of general transfer

Now, in order to understand the first article, you can also draw a mind map.

Unit Project

Work in groups to make research about articles about the way to promote retention and share your findings with freshmen.

1. Find articles about the way to promote retention and sum up their views.
2. Hold a discussion in groups about whether you agree with the views of those articles.
3. Give an analysis of those articles by using Ausubel and Bruner's views.
4. Share your findings in PPT form with freshmen so that they can improve their learning efficiency.